The Third Book of Enoch:

Also called 3 Enoch
and The Hebrew Book of Enoch

By Joseph B. Lumpkin

Joseph B. Lumpkin

The Third Book of Enoch:
Also called 3 Enoch
and The Hebrew Book of Enoch

First time or interested authors, contact Fifth Estate Publishers,
Post Office Box 116, Blountsville, AL 35031.

Second Revision, 2010

Cover Design by An Quigley

Printed on acid-free paper

Library of Congress Control No: 2009912934

ISBN: 9781933580821

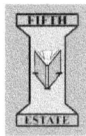

Fifth Estate, 2010

Joseph B. Lumpkin

INTRODUCTION

The study of scripture is a lifelong venture. Many times our search for deeper understanding of the holy book leads to questions beyond the Bible itself. As we encounter references to social conditions, cultural practices, and even other writings mentioned within the scriptures we are called to investigate and expand our knowledge in order to fully appreciate the context, knowledge base, and cultural significance of what is being taught. Thus, to fully understand the Bible, we are necessarily drawn to sources outside the Bible. These sources add to the historical, social, or theological understanding of Biblical times. As our view becomes more macrocosmic, we see the panoramic setting and further understand the full truth within the scriptures.

To point us to the sources we should be concerned with, we must know which books were popular and important at the time. There are several books mentioned in the Bible which are not included in the Bible. They are not spiritual canon, either because they were not available at the time the canon was originally adopted, or at the time they were not considered "inspired." In cases when inspiration was questioned, one could argue that any book quoted or mentioned by a prophet or an apostle should be considered as spiritual canon. Unfortunately this position would prove too simplistic.

Books and writings can fall under various categories such as civil records and laws, historical documents, or spiritual writings. A city or state census is not inspired, but it could add insight into certain areas of life. Spiritual writings which are directly quoted in the Bible serve as insights into the beliefs of the writer or what was considered acceptable by society at the time. As with any new discovery, invention, or belief, the new is interpreted based upon the structure of what came before. This was the way in the first century Christian church as beliefs were based upon the old Jewish understanding. Although, one should realize pagan beliefs were also added to the church as non-Jewish populations were converted, bringing with them the foundations of their beliefs on which they interpreted Christianity. In the case of Jude, James, Paul, and others, the Jewish past was giving way to the Christian present but their understanding and doctrine were still being influenced by what they had learned and experienced previously. It becomes obvious that to understand the Bible one should endeavor to investigate the books and doctrines that most influenced the writers of the Bible.

The Dead Sea Scrolls found in the caves of Qumran are of great interest in the venture of clarifying the history and doctrine in existence between biblical times and the fixing of canon. Many of the scrolls were penned in the second century B.C. and were in use at least until the destruction of the second temple in 70 A.D. Similar scrolls to those found in the eleven caves of Qumran were also found at the Masada stronghold which fell in 73 A.D. Fragments of every book of the Old Testament except Esther were found in the caves of Qumran, but so were many other books. Some of these books are considered to have been of equal importance and influence to the people of Qumran and to the writers and scholars of the time. Some of those studying the scrolls found in Qumran were the writers of the New Testament.

Knowing this, one might ask which of the dozens of non-canonical books most influenced the writers of the New Testament. It is possible to ascertain the existence of certain influences within the Bible context by using the Bible itself. The Bible can direct us to other works in three ways. The work can be mentioned by name, as is the Book of Jasher. The work can be quoted within the Bible text, as is the case with the Book of Enoch. The existence of the work can be alluded to, as is the case of the missing letter from the apostle Paul to the Corinthians.

In the case of those books named in the Bible, one can set a list as the titles are named. The list is lengthier than one might first suspect. Most of these works have not been found. Some have been unearthed but their authenticity is questioned. Others have been found and the link between scripture and scroll is generally accepted. Following is a list of books mentioned in the Holy Bible.

The Book of Jasher: There are two references to the book in the Old Testament:

2 Samuel 1:18 – Also he bade them teach the children of Judah the use of the bow: behold, it is written in the book of Jasher.

Joshua 10:13 - Is it not written in the Book of Jasher? And the sun stopped in the middle of the sky and did not hasten to go down for about a entire day.

There are several books which have come to us entitled, "Book of Jasher." One is an ethical treatise from the Middle Ages. It begins with a section on the Mystery of the Creation of the World: It is clearly unrelated to the Biblical Book of Jasher.

Another was published in 1829 supposedly translated by Flaccus Albinus Alcuinus. It opens with the Chapter 1 Verse 1 reading: "While it was the beginning, darkness overspread the face of nature." It is now considered a fake.

The third and most important is by Midrash, first translated into English in 1840. It opens with Chapter 1 Verse 1 reading: "And God said, Let us make man in our image, after our likeness, and God created man in his own image." A comparison of Joshua 10:13 with Jasher 88:63-64 and 2Sam. 1:18 with Jasher 56:9 makes it clear that this Book of Jasher at least follows close enough with the Bible to be the Book of Jasher mentioned in the Bible. A translation of the Book of Jasher is available by Joseph Lumpkin, published by Fifth Estate.

Other books mentioned by name in the Bible are:

1.   The Book of Wars of the Lord: "Therefore it is said in the Book of the Wars of the Lord." Num. 21:14

2.   The Annals of Jehu: "Now the rest of the acts of Jehoshaphat, first to last, behold, they are written in the annals

of Jehu the son of Hanani, which is recorded in the Book of the Kings of Israel." 2 Chronicles 20:34

3.   The treatise of the Book of the Kings: "As to his sons and the many oracles against him and the rebuilding of the house of God, behold, they are written in the treatise of the Book of the Kings. Then Amaziah his son became king in his place." 2 Chronicles 24:27

4.   The Book of Records, Book of the Chronicles of Ahasuerus: "Now when the plot was investigated and found to be so, they were both hanged on a gallows; and it was written in the Book of the Chronicles in the king's presence." ... "During that night the king could not sleep so he gave an order to bring the book of records, the chronicles, and they were read before the king." Esther 2:23; 6:1

5.   The Acts of Solomon: "Now the rest of the acts of Solomon and whatever he did, and his wisdom, are they not written in the book of the Acts of Solomon?" 1 Kings 11:41

6.   The Sayings of Hozai: "His prayer also and how God was entreated by him, and all his sin, his unfaithfulness, and

the sites on which he built high places and erected the Asherim and the carved images, before he humbled himself, behold, they are written in the records of the Hozai." 2 Chronicles 33:19

7.	The Chronicles of David: "Joab the son of Zeruiah had begun to count them, but did not finish; and because of this, wrath came upon Israel, and the number was not included in the account of the Chronicles of King David." 1 Chronicles 27:24

8.	The Chronicles of Samuel, Nathan, Gad: "Now the acts of King David, from first to last, are written in the Chronicles of Samuel the seer, in the Chronicles of Nathan the prophet and in the Chronicles of Gad the seer." 1 Chronicles 29:29

9.	Samuel's book: "Then Samuel told the people the ordinances of the kingdom, and wrote them in the book and placed it before the Lord." 1 Samuel 10:25

10.	The Records of Nathan the prophet: "Now the rest of the acts of Solomon, from first to last, are they not written in the Records of Nathan the prophet, and in the prophecy of Ahijah the Shilonite, and in the visions of Iddo the seer concerning Jeroboam the son of Nebat?" 2 Chronicles 9:29

11.   The Prophecy of Ahijah the Shilonite: "Now the rest of the acts of Solomon, from first to last, are they not written in the Records of Nathan the prophet, and in the prophecy of Ahijah the Shilonite, and in the visions of Iddo the seer concerning Jeroboam the son of Nebat?" 2 Chronicles 9:29

12.   The Treatise of the Prophet Iddo: "Now the rest of the acts of Abijah, and his ways and his words are written in the treatise of the prophet Iddo." 2 Chronicles 13:22
The existence of a book can be inferred as well, this is clearly seen with several missing epistles.

Paul's letter to the church at Laodicea: "When this letter is read among you, have it also read in the church of the Laodiceans; and you, for your part read my letter that is coming from Laodicea." Colossians 4:16 (Since three earlier manuscripts do not contain the words "at Ephesus" in Eph 1:1, some have speculated that the letter coming from Laodicea was in fact the letter of Ephesians. Apostolic fathers also debated this possibility.)

In Paul's first letter to Corinth, he predated that letter by saying: "I wrote you in my letter not to associate with immoral people" (1 Corinthians 5:9) (This could merely be a reference to the present letter of 1 Corinthians.)

Of all the books quoted, paraphrased, or referred to in the Bible, the First Book of Enoch has influenced the writers of the Bible as few others have. Even more extensively than in the Old Testament, the writers of the New Testament were frequently influenced by other writings, including the Book of 1 Enoch. However, things are never easy when such a span of time is involved. Over the elapsed two-thousand years, three major works attributed to Enoch have been discovered. Because 3 Enoch draws information from and has part of its foundation in the First Book of Enoch, we will touch on 1 Enoch and 2 Enoch, and then introduce 3 Enoch.

It is not the purpose of this work to make judgments as to the validity or worth of the Books of Enoch, but rather to simply put forth a meaningful question. Are not the non-canonical books that most influenced the thought and theology of the writers of the New Testament worth further research and contemplation?

Before we continue in our study of the Books of Enoch there are several questions we must keep in mind. If a book is mentioned or quoted in the Bible is it not worthy of further study? If it is worth investigating, is 1 Enoch the book of which the Bible speaks? Is 3 Enoch an extension of this knowledge? What knowledge or insight does it add to our understanding of the Bible or the men who wrote it? What can it tell us about the people or beliefs of the time?

The Books of Enoch were once cherished by Jews and Christians alike. 1 Enoch is read in certain Coptic Christian Churches in Ethiopia today and is actually part of the Ethiopic Christian Bible.

Three versions of the Book of Enoch exist today. Most scholars date the First Book of Enoch to some time during the second century B.C. We do not know what earlier oral tradition, if any, the book contains. Enoch was considered inspired and authentic by certain Jewish sects of the first century B.C. and remained popular for at least five hundred years. The earliest Ethiopian text was apparently derived from a Greek manuscript of the Book of Enoch, which itself was a copy of an earlier text. The original was apparently written in the Semitic language, now thought to be Aramaic.

The First Book of Enoch was discovered in the 18th century. It was assumed to have been penned after beginning of the Christian era. This theory was based upon the fact that it had quotes and paraphrases as well as concepts found in the New Testament. Thus, it was assumed that it was heavily influenced by writers such as Jude and Peter.

However, recent discoveries of copies of the book among the Dead Sea Scrolls found at Qumran prove the book was in existence long before the time of Jesus Christ. These scrolls force a closer look and reconsideration. It becomes obvious that the New Testament did not influence the Book of Enoch; on the contrary, the First Book of Enoch influenced the New Testament. The date of the original writing upon which the second century B.C. Qumran copies were based is shrouded in obscurity. Likewise lost are the sources of the oral traditions that came to be the First Book of Enoch.

It has been largely the opinion of historians that the book does not really contain the authentic words of the ancient Enoch, since he would have lived several thousand years earlier than the first known appearance of the book attributed to him. However, the first century Christians accepted 1 Enoch (First Book of Enoch) as inspired, if not authentic. They relied on it to understand the origin and purpose of many things, from angels to wind, sun, and stars. In fact, many of the key concepts used by Jesus Christ himself seem directly connected to terms and ideas in the First Book of Enoch.

It is hard to avoid the evidence that Jesus not only studied the book, but also respected it highly enough to allude to its doctrine and content. Enoch is replete with mentions of the coming kingdom and other holy themes. It was not only Jesus who quoted phrases or ideas from Enoch, there are over one hundred comments in the New Testament which find precedence in 1 Enoch.

Other evidence of the early Christians' acceptance of the First Book of Enoch was for many years buried under the King James Bible's mistranslation of Luke 9:35, describing the transfiguration of Christ: "And there came a voice out of the cloud, saying, 'This is my beloved Son. Hear him.' " Apparently the translator here wished to make this verse agree with a similar verse in Matthew and Mark. But Luke's verse in the original Greek reads: "This is my Son, the Elect One (from the Greek ho eklelegmenos, lit., "the elect one"). Hear him."
The "Elect One" is a most significant term (found fourteen times) in the Book of Enoch. If the book was indeed known to

the apostles of Christ, with its abundant descriptions of the Elect One who should "sit upon the throne of glory" and the Elect One who should "dwell in the midst of them;" then the great scriptural authenticity is justly accorded to the Book of Enoch when the "voice out of the cloud" tells the apostles, "This is my Son, the Elect One,"… the one promised in the Book of Enoch.

The Book of Jude tells us in Verse 14 that "Enoch, the seventh from Adam, prophesied." Jude also, in Verse 15, makes a direct reference to the Book of Enoch (2:1), where he writes, "to execute judgment on all, to convict all who are ungodly." As a matter of fact, it is a direct, word for word quote. Therefore, Jude's reference to the Enochian prophesies strongly leans toward the conclusion that these written prophesies were available to him at that time.

Fragments of ten Enoch manuscripts were found among the Dead Sea Scrolls. The number of scrolls indicate the Essenes (a Jewish commune or sect at the time of Christ) could well have used the Enochian writings as a community prayer book or teacher's manual and study text.

Many of the early church fathers also supported the Enochian writings. Justin Martyr ascribed all evil to demons whom he alleged to be the offspring of the angels who fell through lust for women; directly referencing the Enochian writings.

Athenagoras (170 A.D.), regarded Enoch as a true prophet. He describes the angels who "violated both their own nature and their office." In his writings, he goes into detail about the nature of fallen angels and the cause of their fall, which comes directly from the Enochian writings.

Since any book stands to be interpreted in many ways, 1 Enoch posed problems for some theologians. Instead of reexamining their own theology, they sought to dispose of that which went counter to their beliefs. Some of the visions in Enoch are believed to point to the consummation of the age in conjunction with Christ's second coming which took place in A.D. 70 (in the destruction of Jerusalem).

This being the case, it should not surprise us that 1 Enoch was declared a fake and was rejected by Hilary, Jerome, and Augustine. Enoch was subsequently lost to Western Christendom for over a thousand years.

Enoch's "seventy generations" was also a great problem. Many scholars thought it could not be made to stretch beyond the First Century. Copies of Enoch soon disappeared. Indeed, for almost two thousand years we knew only the references made to it in the Bible. Without having the book itself, we could not have known it was being quoted in the Bible, sometimes word for word by Peter and Jude.

"...the Lord, having saved a people out of the land of Egypt, afterward destroyed them that believed not. And angels that kept not their own principality, but left their proper habitation, he hath kept in everlasting bonds under darkness unto the judgment of the great day. Even as Sodom and Gomorrah, and the cities about them...in like manner...are set out as examples...." (Jude 5-7)

"For if God spared not the angels when they sinned, but cast them down into hell, and committed them to pits of darkness, to be reserved unto judgment." (2 Peter 2.4)

To what extent other New Testament writers regarded 1 Enoch as scriptural canon may be determined by comparing their writings with those found in Enoch. A strong possibility of influence upon their thought and choice of wording is evidenced by a great many references found in Enoch which remind one of passages found in the New Testament.

The Books of Enoch seem to be a missing link between Jewish and Christian theology and are considered by many to be more Christian in its theology than Jewish. First Enoch was considered scripture by many early Christians. The literature of the church fathers is filled with references to this book. The early second century apocryphal book of the Epistle of Barnabus makes many references and quotes from the Book of Enoch. Second and third century church fathers like Justin Martyr, Irenaeus, Origin and Clement of Alexandria all seemed to have accepted Enoch as authentic. Tertullian (160-230 A.D.) even called the Book of Enoch, "Holy Scripture". The Ethiopian Coptic Church holds the Book of Enoch as part of its official spiritual canon. It was widely known and read the first three centuries after Christ. This and many other books became discredited after the Council of Laodicea. And being under ban of the authorities, it gradually disappeared from circulation.

In 1773, rumors of a surviving copy of the book drew Scottish explorer James Bruce to distant Ethiopia. He found the Book of Enoch had been preserved by the Ethiopian church, which put it right alongside the other books of the Bible.

Bruce secured not one, but three Ethiopian copies of the book and brought them back to Europe and Britain. In 1773 Bruce returned from six years in Abyssinia. In 1821 Richard Laurence published the first English translation. The famous R.H. Charles edition was published in 1912. In the following years several portions of the Greek text surfaced. Then with the discovery of cave 4 at Qumran, seven fragmentary copies of the Aramaic text were discovered.

Later, another "Book of Enoch" surfaced. This text, dubbed "2 Enoch" or "Second Enoch," and commonly called "the Slavonic Enoch," or "The Secrets of Enoch" was discovered in 1886 by Professor Sokolov in the archives of the Belgrade Public Library. It appears that just as "Ethiopian Enoch" ("1 Enoch") escaped the sixth-century Church suppression of certain texts in the Mediterranean area, so also did "Slavonic Enoch" survive by being propagated in another language long after the original form, from which it was copied, was destroyed or hidden.

Specialists in the Enochian texts believe that the missing original from which the Slavonic was copied was probably a

Greek manuscript, which itself may have been based on a Hebrew or Aramaic manuscript.

The Slavonic text has evidence of many later additions to the original manuscript. Unfortunately, later additions and the deletion rendered the text unreliable.

Because of certain references to dates and data regarding certain calendar systems in the Slavonic Enoch, some claim the text cannot be earlier than the seventh century A.D. Some see these passages not as evidence of Christian authorship, but as later Christian interpolations into an earlier manuscript. Enochian specialist R.H. Charles, for instance, believes that even the better of the two Slavonic manuscripts contains interpolations and is, in textual terms, "corrupt."

The last great book of the Enochian tradition is 3 Enoch or the Hebrew Book of Enoch. 3 Enoch is a wealth of mystical knowledge. The book claims to be authored by Rabbi Ishmael, a highly respected and brilliant priest living between 90 and 130 A.D. however, no fragments have been found dating earlier than around 400 A.D. The book was written in Hebrew but has a few Latin and Greek word and cognates. 3 Enoch has its roots in the Metatron tradition, which has Enoch ascending to heaven and being translated into the angel Metatron. He is then given authority over the angels and the earthly nations, much to the protests of the angelic host. The amount of mystical information, along with the angelology contained in the book is unrivaled. 3 Enoch is obviously a continuation and expansion of the Enochian traditions of 1 and 2 Enoch, which are drawn on for the story's foundation. The complete text of 3 Enoch had been very difficult to find. Usually one finds only fragmentary sources here and there. These various Hebrew language fragments were brought together in a master work in 1928 done at Cambridge, England. Most information on 3 Enoch exists in forms available to scholars but not to the general public. By reinterpreting, augmenting and supplementing the Hebrew text with various sources and articles, an informative document, suitable for the general public was produced. It is with great joy that The Third Book of Enoch is presented in its entirety.

Introduction of 3 Enoch

Author's Note: It was not until the early 1900's that The Hebrew Book of Enoch, or 3 Enoch, could be reconstructed. Although the text claims to be written around 100 A.D. it was likely written by a highly educated Rabbi around 300 to 400 A.D. and preserved only in fragments, here and there. Then, in 1928 Dr. Hugo Odeberg PhD. gathered the various Hebrew fragmentary sources and published the first full translation along with copious scholarly notes, including the source Hebrew material. The University Press at Cambridge, in the United Kingdom, published the book. A photocopy of the book made its way to the United State and into the University of Chicago library, where it was kept for many years. It was from this body of work and from this photocopied and preserved manuscript that some of the Hebrew source of this work was compiled. The material was then compared to and supplemented with dozens of other articles and sources to produce this work.

3 Enoch purports to have been written around 100 A.D., but its origins can only be traced to the late fourth or early fifth centuries. Other names for 3 Enoch include "The Third Book of Enoch" and "The Book of the Palaces." The angelology and

description of heaven in 1 Enoch is built upon and greatly expanded in 3 Enoch.

The book is rife with Hebrew words, which have no single English equivalent. Even though care was taken to define the majority of these words when first they appear in the text, the reader should expect only keywords to replace or augment meanings thereafter. To do otherwise would either leave the reader to remember the meanings of all Hebrew words or bloat the book to the point of making it difficult to follow.

Modern scholars describe this book as belonging to a body of work called the pseudepigraphia. 3 Enoch claims to be written by a Rabbi, who became a 'high priest' after he had visions of an ascension to Heaven, 90 AD - 135 AD. Rabbi Ishmael is a leading figure of Merkabah literature; however, a number of scholars suggest that it was in fact written by a number of people over a prolonged period of time.

Merkabah writings had to do with the theme of ascension into heaven. The name is derived from a Hebrew word meaning "chariot," referring to Ezekiel's vision beginning in Ezekiel 1:4. Enoch's contents and ideas are unique and newer than those shown in other Merkabah texts, suggesting the book may be among the first in the Merkabah movement or that it is derived through unique influences.

Joseph B. Lumpkin

As the other name of this book implies, 3 Enoch is also part of
the Temple or Hekalot body of literature. The name Sefer
Hekhalot means, "Palaces" or "Temples."

 As with 1 Enoch, the exact dating of this book is a difficult
task, but some scholars believe it was completed around the
time of the Babylonian Talmud, which was around the early 5th
century A.D.

3 Enoch was originally written in Hebrew, although it contains
a number of words from both Greek and Latin. Parts of the
book seem to have been influenced by 1 Enoch, showing the
author was familiar with the Mystical Enochian Tradition.

Similar points appearing in 1 Enoch and 3 Enoch are:
  Enoch ascends to Heaven in a storm chariot (3 Enoch 6:1; 7:1)
  Enoch is translated into an angel (3 Enoch 9:1-5; 15:1-2)
  Enoch, as an angel, is given authority in Heaven (3 Enoch 10:1-
3; 16:1)
  Enoch receives an explanation or vision of creation and
cosmology. (3 Enoch 13:1-2)
  Enoch sees a hostile angel named Azazel (3 Enoch 4:6; 5:9)

The main theme, throughout the book is the change or
"transubstantiation" of Enoch into the angel Metatron.

Metatron appears in various Jewish, Christian, and Islamic

works but was a central focus in medieval Jewish mystical texts and occult sources. Rabbinical texts point to Metatron as the angel who stilled the hand of Abraham, preventing him from sacrificing Isaac.

The place and authority of Metatron has been hotly debated, and is seen even within the book. He is seen as sitting in heaven. This is only permitted if one is a deity. He is referred to in the text as "The Lesser YHWH."

YHWH makes up the Tetragrammaton forming the name we pronounce as "Yahweh" or "Jehovah." The four letters making up the divine name are Yodh, He Waw, He, having the sounds of "Y", "H", "W, O, U or a place holder", and "H." When "He" ends a word it is often silent. Due to the fact that German theologians were heavily involved in theological research and study, one may also find the Tetragrammaton rendered as YHVH, since the V in German has a W sound.

There is a very personal attack within the text, which should be explained. A curse is placed on a man known only as Acher. In Hebrew the name means, "the other," and is used as a term of alienation from the rabbinic community. The Talmud tells us that Elisha be Abuyah entered Paradise in a vision and saw Metatron sitting down (an action that in heaven is permitted only to God himself). Elishah ben Abuyah therefore looked to Metatron as a deity and proclaimed, "There are indeed two powers in heaven!" The other rabbis explain that Metatron was allowed to sit because he was the Heavenly Scribe, writing down the deeds of Israel (Babylonian Talmud, Hagiga 15a). The intense hatred for any idea hinting at dualism or polytheism, as opposed to monotheism, caused such a reaction within the Rabbinical community that they labeled Elisha be Abuyah a heretic. In 3 Enoch this point is driven home when the entire nation of Israel is to be reconciled to God, except for Acher, whose name is blotted out.

In spite of the disagreements within the ancient Jewsih community, the reader is still left to wonder what position Metatron occupies in heaven. Metatron is described in two ways: as a primordial angel (9:2–13:2) and as the transformation of Enoch after he was assumed into Heaven, and he is called "The Lesser YHWH."

Enoch walked with God; then he was no more, because God took him away. [Genesis 5:24 NIV.]
This Enoch, whose flesh was turned to flame, his veins to fire, his eye-lashes to flashes of lightning, his eye-balls to flaming torches, and whom God placed on a throne next to the throne of glory, received after this heavenly transformation the name Metatron. [3 Enoch]

As the Christian community came in contact with the Jewish book of 3 Enoch, they had little trouble reconciling the names and position of Metatron. To those Christians a person who may sit in heaven and who judges, and who is called by the same name taken by God must be Yeshua (Jesus.)

It may be of help if the meaning of the name, Metatron, could be ascertained, but it is not clear. Suggestions are that the name originated from the root words of such phrases as, "keeper of the watch," "guard," "to protect," "one who serves behind the throne," "one who occupies the throne next to the throne of glory," "to lead," or " to measure." None of these suggestions can be proven. From the text itself we know only that Metatron is referred to as "the youth," likely because he would be the newest and youngest angel. He is also called, "the prince of the presence (of God)." His purpose in heaven was to be a witness against mankind.

A type of numerology is used and referred to within the text. Temurah is one of the three ancient methods used by Cabbalist to rearrange words and sentences in the Torah, in the belief that by this method they can derive the deeper, hidden spiritual meaning of the words. Temurah may be used to change letters in certain words to create a new meaning for a Biblical statement. Another method is called Gematria. In this method letters are substituted for numbers and the meaning of words with the same value are compared along with the numerical meaning of the words.

A preparatory summery of the first section of the book may be framed as a revelation from Metatron, or the Prince of the Presence, to Rabbi Ishmael. Metatron, as it turns out, is Enoch and this is why the title of this book has come to be called, "3 Enoch." Any question as to who Metatron may be is answered clearly in CHAPTER 4, where it is written, "Rabbi Ishmael said: I asked Metatron and said to him: " why are you called by the name of your Creator, by seventy names? You are greater than all the princes, higher than all the angels, beloved more than all the servants, honored above all the mighty ones in kingship, greatness and glory: why do they call you 'Youth' in the high heavens?" He answered and said to me: "Because I am Enoch, the son of Jared. For when the generation of the flood sinned and were confounded in their deeds, saying unto God: Depart from us, for we desire not the knowledge of your ways (Job 21:14), then the Holy One, blessed be He, removed me from their midst to be a witness against them in the high heavens to all the inhabitants of the world, that they may not say: 'The Merciful One is cruel'.

The following text begins the book of 3 Enoch. Notes and explanations are italicized. Words placed in parentheses are alternate renderings of a word or phrase.

BOOK OF 3 ENOCH

or the Hebrew Book of Enoch

By Rabbi ISHMAEL BEN ELISHA
THE HIGH PRIEST

CHAPTER I

INTRODUCTION: Rabbi Ishmael ascends to heaven to witness the vision of the Merkaba (chariot). He is given to Metatron

AND ENOCH WALKED WITH GOD: AND HE WAS NOT; FOR GOD TOOK HIM.

(1) I ascended on high to witness the vision of the Merkaba (the divine chariot) and I had entered the six Halls, which were situated within one another.

The halls were in concentric circles, one within the other.

(2) As soon as I reached the door of the Seventh Hall I stood still in prayer before the Holy One, blessed be He. I lifted up my eyes on high towards the Divine Majesty and I said: (3) "

Lord of the Universe, I pray you, that the worthiness of Aaron, the son of Amram, who loves and pursues peace, and who received the crown of priesthood from Your Glory on Mount Sinai, be upon me in this hour, so that Khafsiel, (Qafsiel) the prince, and the angels with him may not overcome (overpower) me nor cast me down from the heavens."

Qafsiel or Qaphsiel is an angel of a high order set to guard the seventh hall of heaven

(4) At that moment the Holy One, blessed be He, sent Metatron, his Servant, also called Ebed, to me. He is the angel, the Prince of the Presence. With great joy he spread his wings as he came to meet me in order to save me from their hand. (5) And by his hand he took me so that they could see us, and he said to me: "Enter in peace before the high and exalted King and see the picture of Merkaba (chariot)."

Merkaba (chariot) – Chariot of fire, Chariot of light - Pulled by four Chayot or living creatures, each of which has four wings and the four faces of a man, lion, ox, and eagle.. See Ezekiel 1:4-26. The Bible makes mention of three types of angel found in the Merkaba (chariot) . The first is the "Seraphim" (lit. "burning") angels. These angels appear like flashes of fire continuously ascending and descending.

These "Seraphim" angels powered the movement of the chariot. In the hierarchy of these angels, "Seraphim" are the highest, that is, closest to God, followed by the "Chayot", which are followed by the "Ophanim." The chariot is in a constant state of motion, and the energy behind this movement runs according to this hierarchy. The movement of the "Ophanim" are controlled by the "Chayot" while the movement of the "Chayot" is controlled by the "Seraphim." The movement of all the angels of the chariot are controlled by the "Likeness of a Man" on the Throne.

(6) Then I entered the seventh Hall, and he led me to the camps of Shekina (understanding) and stood me in front of the Holy One, blessed be He, to see the Merkaba (chariot).

Shekina - Shekhinah is derived from a Hebrew verb literally meaning "to settle, inhabit, or dwell." (See Exodus 40:35, "Moses could not enter the Tent of Meeting, for the cloud rested [shakhan] upon it, and the glory of the Lord filled the Tabernacle." See also Genesis 9:27, 14:13, Psalms 37:3, Jeremiah 33:16), as well as the weekly Shabbat blessing recited in the Temple ("May He who causes His name to dwell [shochan] in this House, cause to dwell among you love and brotherliness, peace and friendship"). Also see Talmud Ketubot 85b). Shekina can also mean royalty or royal residence. Shekina has come to mean the effect or manifestation caused by the presence or inhabitation of God. The manifestation is glory, creativity, and understanding. These words may be used to explain "Shekina."

(7) As soon as the princes of the Merkaba (chariot) and the flaming Seraphim knew I was there, they fixed their gaze on me. Trembling and shuddering seized me at once and I fell down and was numbed by the brightness of the vision of their faces; until the Holy One, blessed be He, chastised them, saying: (8)" My servants, my Seraphim, my Cherubim and my Ophannim! Cover your eyes before Ishmael, my son, my friend, my beloved one and (my) glory, so that he ceases trembling and shaking! "

The root of Seraphim comes either from the Hebrew verb saraph ('to burn') or the Hebrew noun saraph (a fiery, flying serpent). Because the term appears several times with reference to the serpents encountered in the wilderness (Num. 21.8, Deut. 8.15; Isa. 14.29; 30.6), it has often been understood to refer to "fiery serpents." From this it has also often been proposed that the seraphim were serpentine in form and in some sense "fiery" creatures or associated with fire.
It is said that whoever lays eyes on a Seraph, he would instantly be incinerated due to the immense brightness of the Seraph.
Cherubs are described as winged beings. The biblical prophet Ezekiel describes the cherubim as a tetrad of living creatures, each having

four faces: of a lion, an ox, an eagle, and a man. They are said to have the stature and hands of a man, the feet of a calf, and four wings. Two of the wings extended upward, meeting above and sustaining the throne of God; while the other two stretched downward and covered the creatures themselves.

Ophanim are described in 1 Enoch as never sleeping. They watch and guard the throne of God. The word ophan means "wheel" in Hebrew. For this reason the Ophanim have been associated with the chariot in Ezekiel and Daniel. It is mentioned as gagal, traditionally "the wheels of gagallin", in "fiery flame" and "burning fire" of the four, eye-covered wheels, each composed of two nested wheels, that move next to the winged Cherubim, beneath the throne of God. The four wheels move with the Cherubim because the spirit of the Cherubim is in them. These are also referred to as the "many-eyed ones" in 2 Enoch. The Ophanim are also equated as the "Thrones", and associated with the "Wheels", in the vision of Daniel 7:9. They carry the throne of God, hence the name.

This may be a good time to explain the singular and plural in Hebrew. Whereas in English we add an "s" to denote a plural, in Hebrew an "im" is added. Thus, there is one Cherub but many Cherubim. There is one Seraph but many Seraphim. Knowing this fact may make the text easier to follow.

(9) Then Metatron, the Prince of the Presence, came and placed my spirit in me again and he stood me up on my feet. (10) After that (moment) for an hour I did not have enough strength to sing a song before the Throne of Glory of the Glorious King, the mightiest of all kings, the most excellent of all princes. (11) After an hour had passed the Holy One, blessed be He, opened the gates of Shekina (understanding) to me. These are the gates of Peace, and of Wisdom, and of Strength, and of Power, and of Speech (Dibbur), and of Song, and of Kedushah (Sacred Salutation of Holy, Holy, Holy), and the gates of Chanting. (12) And he opened and shined His light in my eyes and my heart by words of psalm, song, praise, exaltation, thanksgiving, extolment, glorification, hymn and eulogy (to speak well of). And as I opened my mouth, singing a song before the Holy One, blessed be He the Holy Chayoth beneath and above the Throne of Glory answered and said (chanted the prayer): "HOLY!" "BLESSED BE THE GLORY OF YHWH FROM HIS PLACE!."

The Chayot (or Chayyot) are a class of Merkabah, or Jewish Mystical Angels, reported in Ezekeil's vision of the Merkabah and its surrounding angels as recorded in the first chapter of the Book of Ezekiel describing his vision by the river Chebar.

Kedushah (Sacred Salutation of Holy, Holy, Holy) is a call to greet and glorify God. KODOISH, KODOISH, KODOISH ADONAI 'TSEBAYOTH: "Holy, Holy, Holy, is the Lord God of Hosts." This is the Sacred Salutation, the Kedushah (Sacred Salutation of Holy, Holy, Holy) , which is used by all the heavenly hosts to worship The Father before His Throne.

CHAPTER 2

The highest classes of angels make inquiries about Rabbi Ishmael, which are answered by Metatron

Rabbi Ishmael said:

(1) Within the hour the eagles of The Chariot (Merkaba), the flaming Ophannim and the Seraphim of consuming fire asked Metatron: (2) "Youth! Why do you permit one born of woman to enter and see the chariot (Merkaba)? From which nation and from which tribe is this one? What is his nature?" (3) Metatron answered and said to them: "From the nation of Israel whom the Holy One, blessed be He, chose for his people from among seventy tongues (nations of the world). He is from the tribe of Levi, whom He set aside as a contribution to his name. He is from the seed of Aaron whom the Holy One, blessed be He,

chose for his servant and He put upon him the crown of priesthood on Sinai." (4) Then they spoke and said: "Happy is the people (nation) that is in that position!" (Ps. 144:15).

CHAPTER 3

Metatron has 70 names, but God calls him 'Youth'

Rabbi Ishmael said:

(1) In that hour I asked Metatron, the angel, the Prince of the Presence: "What is your name?" (2) He answered me: "I have seventy names, corresponding to the seventy nations of the world and all of them are based upon the name Metatron, angel of the Presence; but my King calls me 'Youth' (Naar)."

Seventy tongues represent the seventy nations or the entirety of the known world.

It is likely the word "youth" is used because Metatron is the newest and youngest being in heaven.

The seventy names are derived from the divine name or the Tetragrammaton – YHWH. Yah is a shortened version of this, meaning "God."

CHAPTER 4

Metatron is Enoch who was translated to heaven at the time of the flood.

Rabbi Ishmael said:

(1) I asked Metatron and said to him: "why does your Creator call you by seventy names? You are greater than all the princes, higher than all the angels, beloved more than all the servants, honored above all the mighty ones in kingship, greatness and glory, so why do they in the high heavens call you 'Youth'? (2) He answered and said to me: "Because I am Enoch, the son of Jared. (3) When the generation of the flood sinned and were twisted and contorted in their deeds, saying unto God: "Depart from us! We do not want the knowledge of your ways," (See Job 21:14), then the Holy One, blessed be He, removed me from their midst so that I could be a witness against them in the high heavens to all the inhabitants of the world, so that they can not say: 'The Merciful One is cruel'. (4) "What sin did all those throngs of their wives, their sons and their daughters, their horses, their mules and their cattle and their property, and all the birds of the world commit so that the Holy One, blessed be He, destroyed the world, together with them in the waters of the flood?" They cannot say: "What in the

generation of the flood sinned and what sin did they do so that the beasts and the birds should perish with them?" (5) Then the Holy One, blessed be He, lifted me up in their lifetime in their sight to be a witness against them to the future world. And the Holy One, blessed be He, assigned me to be a prince and a ruler among the ministering angels.

This chapter lays out the purpose of 3 Enoch and why it is so named. Metatron confirms that he is indeed Enoch, who was taken to heaven, translated into the being, Metatron, His primary purpose was to be a witness against man's sin on earth. When man or angel asked what sin was committed that all on earth should be destroyed, Enoch, now known as Metatron, would be a witness.

(6) In that hour three of the ministering angels, UZZA, 'AZZA and AZZAEL came out and accused me in the high heavens in front of the Holy One, blessed be He: And they said, "The Progenitors, The Ancient Ones, said before You with justification: Do not create man! The Holy One, blessed be He, answered and said unto them: "I have made and I will bear, and yes, I will carry and will deliver." (7) As soon as they saw me, they said before Him: "Lord of the Universe! What is this one that he should ascend to the highest heights? Is he not one from among the sons of those who perished in the days of the

Flood? What is he doing in the Raqia (firmament / heavens)."
What business does he have being in heaven?

Some sources have the names of the angels include Mal'aki or Mamlaketi. Azzael is one of the ten heads of the heavenly Sanhedrin. Rabbinical sources have Azza and Azzael as giants. All three are said to be agents of evil who accuse man of sins. These are the fallen angels. Another theory is that Azza and Azzael are not individual angels but are orders of angels.

Raquia is a key Hebrew word in Genesis 1:6–8a. It is translated "firmament" in the King James Version and "expanse" in most Hebrew dictionaries and modern translations. Raqa means to spread out, beat out, or hammer as one would a malleable metal. It can also mean "plate." The Greek Septuagint translated raqia 16 out of 17 times with the Greek word stereoma, which means "a firm or solid structure." The Latin Vulgate (A.D. 382) used the Latin term "firmamentum," which also denotes solidness and firmness. The King James translators coined the word "firmament" because there was no single word equivalent in English. Today, "firmament" is usually used poetically to mean sky, atmosphere, or heavens. In modern Hebrew, raqia means sky or heavens. However, originally it probably meant something solid or firm that was spread out.

Azzael is likely the same being as Azazel, the accuser angel who was the leader of the fallen ones. Etymology connects the word with the mythological "Uza" and "Azael", the fallen angels, to whom a reference is believed to be found in Gen. 6:2,4. In accordance with this etymology, the sacrifice of the goat atones for the sin of fornication of which those angels were guilty. (See 1 Enoch.) Leviticus 16:8-10: "and Aaron shall cast lots upon the two goats, one lot for the Lord and the other lot for Azazel. And Aaron shall present the goat on which the lot fell for the Lord, and offer it as a sin offering; but the goat on which the lot fell for Azazel shall be presented alive before the Lord to make atonement over it, that it may be sent away into the wilderness to Azazel."

(8) Again, the Holy One, blessed be He, answered and said to them: "What are you, that you enter and speak in my presence? I delight more in this one than in all of you put together, and therefore he will be a prince and a ruler over you in the high heavens." (9) Then they all stood up and went out to meet me, and bowed themselves down before me and said: "Happy are you and happy is your father for your Creator favors you." (10) And because I am small and a youth among them in days, months and years, therefore they call me "Youth" (Na'ar).

CHAPTER 5

The idolatry of the generation of Enosh causes God to remove
the Shekina from earth. Idolatry was inspired by Azza, Uzza
and Azzael

Rabbi Ishmael said: Metatron, the Prince of the Presence, said
to me:

(1) From the day when the Holy One, blessed be He, evicted
the first Adam from the Garden of Eden, and continuing from
that day, the Shekina (glory) was dwelling upon a Cherub
under the Tree of Life. (2) And the ministering angels were
gathering together and going down from heaven in groups.
From the Raqia (heaven) they went in companies from the
heavens in camps to perform His will in the entire world. (3)
And the first man and his children were sitting outside the gate
of the Garden to see the glowing, bright appearance of the
Shekina (glory). (4) For the splendor of the Shekina (glory)
enfolds the world from end to end with its splendor 365,000
times that of the orb of the sun. And everyone who made use
of the splendor of the Shekina, on him no flies and no gnats lit,
and he was not ill and he suffered no pain. No demons could
overpower him, neither were they able to injure him. (5) When

the Holy One, blessed be He, went out and went in from the
Garden to Eden, from Eden to the Garden, from the Garden to
Raqia (heaven) and from Raqia (heaven) to the Garden of Eden
then everything and everyone saw His magnificent Shekina
and they were not injured; (6) until the time of the generation
of Enosh who was the head of all idol worshippers of the
world.

The Shekina was an energy or substance that was protecting those
who used it from illness, demons, and even bugs.

(7) And what did the generation of Enosh do? They went from
one end of the world to the other, and each person brought
silver, gold, precious stones and pearls in heaps the size of
mountains and hills to make idols out of them throughout the
entire world. And they erected the idols in every corner of the
world: the size of each idol was 1000 parasangs.

The generations of Enoch are as follows: Adam, Seth, Enosh, Kenan,
Mahalalel, Jared, Enoch.
The highest (worst) sins, according to Rabbis, are idolatry, adultery,
bloodshed, and sorcery and calling God's name in vain.
A parasang is a length or measurement of distance used in what is
now Iran. It varied according to the region. The north-eastern

parasang was about 15,000 paces, the north-western parasang was 18,000 paces, and the one of the south-west was merely 6,000 paces. The measurement called the "true parasang" was about 9,000 paces.

(8) And they brought down the sun, the moon, planets and constellations, and placed them in front of the idols on the right side and on the left side of the idols, to attend to them just like they attend the Holy One, blessed be He, for it is written (I Kings 22:19): "And all the hosts of heaven were standing by him on his right hand and on his left." (9) What power was in them to enable to bring them down? They would not have been able to bring them down, if it had not been for the fact that UZZA, and AZZIEL (other sources have Azzael) taught them sorceries by which they brought them down and enslaved them.

It is obvious that the actual sun and stars were not brought down, but the angelic powers controlling them were summoned. Also, keep in mind that some cultures thought stars to be evil angels who flew across the sky. These agents were summoned and used.

(10) In that time the ministering angels accused them before the Holy One, blessed be He, saying: "Master of the World! Why do you bother with the children of men? As it is written (Ps.

8:4) 'What is man (Adam) that you are mindful of him?' But it was not about Adam that this was written but about Enosh, for he is the head of the idol worshippers. (11) Why have you left the highest of the high heavens which are filled with the majesty of your glory and are high, lifted up, and exalted on the high and exalted throne in the Raqia (heaven) of Araboth (highest heaven) and are gone and dwell with the children of men who worship idols and equate you to (place you on the same level as) the idols.

The word "Araboth (highest heaven)" occurs in Psalm 68:4 `Extol him who rides upon the Araboth (highest heaven)' in which it is usually translated simply as the highest heaven. In the case of 3 Enoch, this would be the throne of God. In the Zoharic commentary on Exodus it is referred to thus: `Be glad in the presence of him who rides upon that concealed heaven which is supported by the Chayoth. The Zohar also interprets the word to mean `mixture' because, it says, this heaven is a mixture of fire and water. This is a mystical statement of a place containing opposites, and thus everything.

(12) Now you are on earth just like the idols. What have you to do with the inhabitants of the earth who worship idols? (13) Then the Holy One, blessed be He, lifted up His Shekina from the earth, from their midst (14) In that moment the ministering

angels came. They are troops of the host and the armies of Araboth (highest heaven) in thousand camps and ten thousand host. They brought trumpets and took the horns in their hands and surrounded the Shekina with all kinds of songs. And He ascended to the high heavens, for it is written (Ps. 47:5) "God is gone up with a shout, the Lord with the sound of a trumpet."

Here the presence and dwelling of God is the Shekina. When the Shekina was taken, God himself left them and took his glory because of idolatry.

CHAPTER 6

Enoch is lifted up to heaven together with the Shekina.

Rabbi Ishmael said: Metatron, the Angel, the Prince of the Presence, said to me:

(1) When the Holy One, blessed be He, wanted to lift me up on high, He first sent Anaphiel YHWH, the Prince, and he took me from their company out of their sight and carried me away in great glory on a chariot of fire pulled by horses of fire, and servants of glory. And he lifted me up to the high heavens

together with the Shekina. (2) As soon as I reached the high heavens, the Holy Chayoth, the Ophannim, the Seraphim, the Cherubim, the Wheels of the Merkaba (chariot) (the Galgallim), and the ministers of the consuming fire, all smelled my scent from a distance of 365,000 myriads of parasangs, and said: "What smells like one born woman and what tastes like a white drop? Who is this that ascends on high. He is merely a gnat among those who can divide flames of fire?"

Chayot are considered angels of fire, who hold up the throne of God and the earth itself.
The angel smells the scent of human, which he finds revolting. He can taste it is the air. The white drop refers to semen. This is an extremely hateful and distasteful statement for the angel to make.

The Holy One, blessed be He, answered and spoke to them: "My servants, my host, my Cherubim, my Ophannim, my Seraphim! Do not be displeased on account of this! Since all the children of men have denied me and my great Kingdom and have all gone worshipping idols, I have removed my Shekina from among them and have lifted it up on high. But this one whom I have taken from among them is an Elect One among (the inhabitants of) the world and he is equal to all of them (put together) in his faith, righteousness and perfection of deed and I have taken him as a tribute from my world under all the heavens.

The statement of "taking a tribute" can be better understood if one looks at Enoch as the best mankind has to offer and God took him as a an act of admiration indicating the intended worth of mankind, had they not turned away from him. The term "Elect One" is very important. It occurs in 1 Enoch and in certain scripture regarding Christ.

CHAPTER 7

Enoch is raised upon the wings of Shekina to the place of the Throne

Rabbi Ishmael said: Metatron, the Angel, the Prince of the Presence, said to me: When the Holy One, blessed be He, took me away from the generation of the Flood, he lifted me on the wings of the wind of Shekina (his glory/understanding) to the highest heaven and brought me to the great palaces of the Araboth (highest heaven) in Raqia (heaven), where the glorious Throne of Shekina, the Merkaba (chariot), the troops of anger, the armies of vehemence, the fiery Shin'anim (accusers), and the flaming Cherubim, the burning Ophanim, the flaming servants, the flashing Chashmallin, the lightning Seraphim live. And he placed me (there) to attend daily to the Throne of Glory.

In some Jewish mystical writings the attributes of Elijah and those of Enoch are interchangeable. Here Enoch takes the same trip to heaven on a fiery chariot.

Here we have various classes of angels, on which we have little information. The Chashmallin are one of the ten classes, which are sometimes silent for a time in heaven. They cease speaking or singing when "The Word" emanates from the throne.

Shin'anim are a class of angel seen in lists of angelic orders. Their name seems to come from a word for "accuser" and thus could be the satans in heaven.

CHAPTER 8

The gates of heaven opened to Metatron

Rabbi Ishmael said: Metatron, the Prince of the presence, said to me:

(1) Before he appointed me to attend the Throne of Glory, the Holy One, blessed be He, opened to me

three hundred thousand gates of Understanding

three hundred thousand gates of Wisdom

three hundred thousand gates of Life

three hundred thousand gates of Grace and Loving-kindness

three hundred thousand gates of Love

three hundred thousand gates of The Torah

three hundred thousand gates of Meekness

three hundred thousand gates of Steadfastness

three hundred thousand gates of Mercy

three hundred thousand gates of Respect for heaven

Other readings add three hundred thousand gates of Shekina, three hundred thousand gates of fear of sin, three hundred thousand gates of power. The gates of steadfastness is also rendered as maintenance and refers to the sustenance to maintain life. All of man's needs come from heaven. Subtlety is rendered as wisdom but includes diplomacy, and craftiness.

(2) Within the hour the Holy One, blessed be He, gave me additional wisdom and to wisdom He added understanding unto understanding, cunning unto cunning, knowledge unto knowledge, mercy unto mercy, instruction unto instruction,

love unto love, loving-kindness unto loving-kindness, goodness unto goodness, meekness unto meekness, power unto power, strength unto strength, might unto might, brightness unto brightness, beauty unto beauty, splendor unto splendor, and I was honored and adorned with all these good praiseworthy things more than all the children of heaven.

Enoch has become more blessed or equipped than "all the children of heaven. Loving-kindness equates to "Grace" of the New Testament.

CHAPTER 9

Enoch receives blessings from the Most High and is adorned with angelic attributes

Rabbi Ishmael said: Metatron, the Prince of the Presence, said to me: (1) After all these things the Holy One, blessed be He, put His hand on me and blessed me with 5360 blessings. (2) And I was raised up and grew to the size of the length and width of the world. (3) And he caused 72 wings to grow on me, 36 on each side. And each wing covered the entire world. (4) And He attached to me 365 eyes: each eye was as the great luminary (moon?). (5) And He left no kind of splendor, brilliance, radiance, beauty of all the lights of the universe that He did not affix to me.

There is no direct correlation for the number 5360. It is not evenly divisible by any other number in the chapter, but it is thought to reflect the number 365, the number of days in a solar year. The number 72 is used to reflect the number of the nations of the world and represents the known world. This is backed up by the phrase stating the wings cover the world.

CHAPTER 10

God places Metatron on a throne as ruler in the seventh Hall.

Rabbi Ishmael said: Metatron, the Prince of the Presence, said to me: (1) All these things the Holy One, blessed be He, made for me. He made me a Throne, similar in form and substance to the Throne of Glory. And He spread a curtain of magnificently bright appearance over me. And it was of beauty, grace, and mercy, similar to the curtain of the Throne of the Glory; and on it were affixed all kinds of lights in the universe.

The idea of a curtain could represent the divine secrets and processes unknown and not available to others.

(2) And He placed the curtain at the door of the Seventh Hall and sat me down on it. (3) And the announcement went forth into every heaven, saying: "This is Metatron, my servant. I have made him a prince and ruler over all the princes of my kingdoms and over all the children of heaven, except the eight great, honored, and revered princes who are the ones called YHWH, by the name of their King."

The eight beings who are called YHWH may refer to those angels who have the Tetragrammaton as part of their name. These are highly ranked angels that are outside the normal system of authority. They are the ones God uses as his counsel.

(4) "And every angel and prince who has a word to speak to me shall now go before him and they shall speak to him instead of Me. (5) And every command that he speaks to you in my name, you will obey, carry out, and fulfill. (Some sources add "Beware of him and do not provoke him.") For the Prince of Wisdom and the Prince of Understanding have I committed to him to instruct him in the wisdom of heavenly things and earthly things, in the wisdom of this world and of the world to

come. (6) Moreover, I have set him over all the storehouses of the palaces of Araboth (highest heaven) and over all the storehouses (reserves) of life that I have in the high heavens."

CHAPTER 11

God reveals all of the great mysteries to Metatron

Rabbi Ishmael said: Metatron, the angel, the Prince of the Presence, said to me:

(1) The Holy One, blessed be He, began revealing to me all the mysteries of Torah and all the secrets of wisdom and the deep mysteries of the Perfect Law. He revealed the thoughts of all living beings and their feelings and all the secrets of the universe and all the secrets of creation. All these were revealed to me just as they are known to the Maker of Creation. (2) And I watched intently to see and understand the secrets and depths of the wonderful mystery. Before a man thought a thought in secret, I saw it and before a man made a thing I watched it. (3) And there was nothing on high or in the depth of the world that was hidden from me.

Here Metatron is given the omniscient power of God.

CHAPTER 12

God puts a crown on him and calls him "the Lesser YHWH"

Rabbi Ishmael said: Metatron, the Prince of the Presence, said to me: (1) Because of the love that the Holy One, blessed be He, loved me with, was more than all the children of heaven, He made me a garment of glory on which were affixed lights all varieties, and He clothed me in it. (2) And He made me a robe of honor on which were affixed beauty, magnificent brilliance and majesty of all sorts. (3) And he made me a crown of royalty on which were affixed forty-nine stones of worth, which were like the light of the orb of the sun.

Forty-nine is a mystical number of seven sevens. The number seven represents spiritual perfection.

(4) Its splendor went out into the four coners of the Araboth (highest heaven) of Raqia (heaven), and through the seven heavens, and throughout the four corners of the world. He

placed it on my head. (5) And He called me THE LESSER
YHWH in the presence of all His heavenly household; for it is
written (Ex. 22: 21): " For my name is in him."

*Without delving too deeply into Jewish mysticism, it should be
pointed out that the numerical value (gematria) of the name Metatron
and that of Shahhdai are the same.*

CHAPTER 13

God writes with a flaming pen on Metatron's crown the letters
by which heaven and earth were created

Rabbi Ishmael said: Metatron, the angel, the Glory of all
heavens and the Prince of the Presence, , said to me: (1) Holy
One, blessed be He, loved and cherished me with great love
and mercy, more than all the children of heaven. Thus, He
wrote with his finger with a flaming pen on the crown upon
my head the letter by which heaven and earth, the seas and
rivers, the mountains and hills, the planets and constellations,
the lightning, winds, earthquakes and thunders, the snow and
hail, the wind of the storm and the tempest were created. These
are the letters by which all the needs of the world and all the

orders of Creation were created. (2) And every single letter flashed out time after time like lightning, and time after time like lanterns, time after time like flames of fire, time after time rays like those of the rising of the sun and the moon and the planets.

There are 22 letters in the Hebrew alphabet. It is thought that all things were created when God spoke the words in the Hebrew tongue. These words are symbolized by the combinations of the 22 letters.

CHAPTER 14

All the highest of the princes and lowest angels fear and tremble at the sight of Metatron crowned.

Rabbi Ishmael said: Metatron, the Angel, the Prince of the Presence, said to me: (1) When the Holy One, blessed be He, put this crown on my head, all the Princes of Nations who are in the height of Araboth (highest heaven) of Raqia (heaven) and all the host of every heaven and even the prince of the Elim, the princes of the 'Er'ellim and the princes of the Tafsarim, who are greater than all the ministering angels who minister before the

Throne of Glory, trembled before me. They shook, feared and trembled before me when they looked at me.

This is a very interesting list of angels and princes. According to Jewish mystical sources, such as the Zohar, there are ten classes of angels under Mikael (Michael). The Er'ellim denotes a general class of angels, while the Elim minster before God in the high heavens. The Tafsarim are the princes of the Elim.

(2) Even Sammael, the Prince of the Accusers, who is greater than all the princes of Nations on high, feared me and shook before me.

Sammael is the head of the satans or accusers. He is also the ruling angel over Rome, the archenemy of Israel.

(3) And even the angel of fire, and the angel of hail, and the angel of wind, and the angel of the lightning, and the angel of wrath, and the angel of the thunder, and the angel of the snow, and the angel of the rain; and the angel of the day, and the angel of the night, and the angel of the sun, and the angel of the moon, and the angel of the planets, and the angel of the constellations whose hands rule the world, all of them feared and shook and were frightened when they looked at me. (4)

These are the names of the rulers of the world: Gabriel, the angel of fire, Baradi-el, the angel who controls hail, Ruchi-el who controls the wind, Baraqi-el who controls the lighting, Zahafi-el who controls the winds of the storm, Rahami-el who controls the thunders, Rahashi-el who controls the earthquake, Shalgiel who controls the snow, Matari-el who controls the rain, Shimshi-el who controls the planets, Rahati-el who controls the constellations. (5) And they all fell to the ground and bowed, when they saw me. And they were not able to look at me because of the majestic glory of the crown on my head.

CHAPTER 15

Metatron is transformed into fire

Rabbi Ishmael said: Metatron, the angel, the Prince of the Presence, and the Glory of all heavens, said to me: (1) As soon as the Holy One, blessed be He, took me into (His) service to attend the Throne of Glory and the Wheels (Galgallim) of the Merkaba (chariot) and the service of Shekina, suddenly my flesh was changed into flames, my muscles into flaming fire, my bones into coals of juniper wood, the light of my eye-lids into hot flames, and all of my limbs into wings of burning fire and my entire body into glowing fire.

Galgallim (sometimes spelled Galgalim) are a high-ranking order of angels, the equivalent of Seraphim. They are metaphorically called "the wheels of the Merkabah" (the 'divine chariot' used to connect people to the divine) and are considered the equivalent of the Orphanim (Cherubim). Galgalim is Hebrew for "wheels."

(2) And on my right flames were burning and dividing, on my left staves of wood (burning staves) were burning, around me the winds of storms and tempests were blowing and in front of me and behind me was roaring thunder accompanied by earthquakes.

CHAPTER 15 - B

This chapter does not occur in all manuscripts. It seems to be a later addition.

Rabbi Ishmael said me: Metatron, the Prince of the Presence and the prince ruling over all the princes, stands before Him who is greater than all the Elohim. And he enters in under the

Throne of Glory. And he has a great dwelling of light on high. And he brings into existence the fire of deafness and places it in the ears of the Holy Chayoth, so that they cannot hear the voice of the Word that sounds from the mouth of the Divine Majesty.

This may indicate that he goes into the holy of holies where he worships and has his own sanctuary.

The idea of more than one Elohim is not new. It is addressed in Psalm 82:

1, The Psalm of Asaph. God stands in the council of the gods; he judges among the gods. 2. How long will you judge unjustly, and show preference to the wicked? Selah. 3. Judge the poor and the orphans; do righteousness to the afflicted and dispossessed. 4. Deliver the poor and oppressed; save them from the hand of the evil. 5. They do not know and they have no understanding; they walk about in darkness. All the foundations of the earth are shaken. 6. I said, "You are gods, and children of Elyon, every one of you." 7. But you will die like mortals, and fall like one of the princes. 8. Rise up, O God, and judge the earth, for you have inherited all the nations.

This section seems to preserve a fragment of a book called, "The Ascension of Moses." The chashmal is the highest point of heaven. It is like a zenith line out of which a window opens.

(2) And when Moses ascended on high, he fasted 121 fasts, until the places where the chashmal live were opened to him; and he saw that the place was as white as a Lion's heart and he saw the companies of the host round about him, which could not be counted. And they wished to burn him. But Moses prayed for mercy, first for Israel and then for himself: and He who was sitting on the Merkaba (chariot) opened the windows above the heads of the Cherubim. And a host of 1800 helpers along with the Prince of the Presence, Metatron, all went out to meet Moses. They took the prayers of Israel and placed them like a crown on the head of the Holy One, blessed be He.

(3) The they said (Deut. 6:4): "Hear, O Israel; the Lord our God is one Lord." And their face were shining and they rejoiced over Shekina and they said to Metatron: "What are these? And to whom do they give all honor and glory?" And they answered: "To the Glorious Lord of Israel." And they spoke: Hear, O Israel: the Lord, our God is one Lord. To Who else shall be given this abundance of honor and majesty but to You YHWH, the Divine Majesty, the King, the living and eternal one." (4) In that moment Akatriel Ya Yehod Sebaoth (a name of the most high) spoke and said to Metatron, the Prince of the Presence and said, "Let no prayer that he prays before me return to him empty (not done). Hear his prayer and fulfill his desire whether it is great or small (5) Then Metatron, the Prince

of the presence, said to Moses, "Son of Amram! Do not be afraid. God delights in you. He asks you what you desire from the Glory and Majesty. Your face shines from one end of the world to the other." But Moses answered him: "I fear that I should bring guiltiness upon myself." Metatron said to him, "Receive the letters of the oath, which makes a covenant that cannot be broken."

Metatron is moving through time to and from the time of Moses. The letters make up the divine names, which are eternal.

CHAPTER 16

This continues the additional material.

His privilege of presiding on a Throne are taken.

Rabbi Ishmael said: Metatron, the Angel, the Prince of the Presence, the Glory of all heaven, said to me: (1) At first I was sitting on a large Throne at the door of the Seventh Hall. There, by authority of the Holy One, blessed be He, I was judging the children of heaven and the servants on high. And I judged Greatness, Kingship, Dignity, Rulership, Honor and Praise, and the Diadem and Crown of Glory for all the princes of kingdoms. While I was presiding in the Court of the Sky (Yeshiba), the princes of nations were standing before me, on my right and on my left, by authority of the Holy One, blessed be He. (2) But when Acher came to see the vision of the Merkaba (chariot) and locked his eyes on me, he was afraid and shook before me so much that his soul was departing from him, because of fear, horror and dread of me, when he saw me sitting upon a throne like a king with all the ministering angels standing by my side serving me and all the princes of kingdoms adorned with crowns all around me. (3) At that moment he opened his mouth and said, "Surely there are two Divine Powers in heaven!" (4) Then the Divine Voice went out from heaven from the Shekina and said: "Return, you backsliding children (Jer.3:22), except for Acher!" (5) Then Anieyel came (Other sources have "Anaphiel YHWH), the Prince, the honored, glorified, beloved, wonderful, revered and fearful one, as ordered by the Holy One, blessed be He and beat me sixty times with whips of fire and made me stand to my feet.

Anieyel , or Anaphiel YHWH is higher in status than Metatron. It is possible the Anieyel is the angel who punishes. The purpose of this chapter is to refute the heresy of the Rabbi called Acher, who believed that there were now two deities in heaven, God and Metatron. To show Metatron is not a deity God sends in a higher angel to take him off his throne and beat him, proving Metatron is not God, nor is he a god. The chapter goes on to call all of Israel to return to God, except for Acher, who has committed an unforgivable sin against the monotheists and against God.

CHAPTER 17

The princes of the seven heavens, and of the sun, moon, planets and constellations.

Rabbi Ishmael said: Metatron, the angel, the Prince of the Presence, the glory of all heavens, said to me: (1) The number of princes are seven. They are the great, beautiful, wonderful, honored, and revered ones. They are assigned over the seven heavens, And these are they: MIKAEL (Michael), GABRIEL, SHATQIEL, BAKARIEL, BADARIEL, PACHRIEL. (Some sources omit Parchriel and add Sidriel.) (2) And every one of them is the prince of the host of one heaven. And each one of them is accompanied by 496,000 groups of ten-thousand ministering angels.

496 is the numerical value of the word Malkut (kingdom). These 496,000 angels are the ones who sing of the glory of God, singing "Holy, Holy. Holy."

(3) MIKAEL is the great prince assigned to ruler over the seventh heaven, the highest one, which is in the Araboth (highest heaven). Gabriel is the prince of the host assigned to rule over the sixth heaven which is in Makon. SHATAQIEL is the prince of the host assigned to rule over the fifth heaven which is in Makon. SHAHAQIEL is the prince of the host assigned to rule over the fourth heaven which is in Zebul. BADARIEL is the prince of the host assigned to rule over the third heaven which is in Shehaqim. BARAKIEL is the prince of the host assigned to rule over the second heaven which is in the height of Raqia (heaven). PAZRIEL is the prince of the host assigned to rule over the first heaven which is in Wilon (or Velum, as the first heaven is called), which is in Shamayim. (4) Under them in GALGALLIEL, the prince who is assigned as ruler over the orb (galgal) of the sun, and with him are 96 great and revered angels who moves the sun in Raqia (heaven) a distance of 365,000 parasangs each day. (5) Under them is OPHANNIEL, the prince who is set the globe (Ophan) of the moon. And with him are 88 (some have it as 68) angels who move the globe of the moon 354 thousand parasangs every

night at the time when the moon stands in the East at its turning point. And the moon is situated in the East at its turning point in the fifteenth day of every month. (6) Under them is RAHATIEL, the prince who is appointed to rule over the constellations. He is accompanied by 72 great and revered angels. And why is he called RAHATIEL? Because he makes the stars run (marhit) in their orbits and courses, which is 339 thousand parasangs every night from the East to West, and from West to East. The Holy One, blessed be He, has made a tent for all of them, for the sun, the moon, the planets and the stars, and they travel in it at night from the West to the East. (7) Under them is KOKBIEL, the prince who is assigned to rule over all the planets. And with him are 365,000 groups of ten-thousand ministering angels, great and revered ones who move the planets from city to city and from province to province in Raqia (the heaven) of heavens. (8) And ruling over them are seventy-two princes of nations (kingdoms) on high corresponding to the 72 nations of the world. And all of them are crowned with crowns of royalty and clothed in royal clothes and wrapped in royal robes. And all of them are riding on royal horses and holding royal scepters in their hands. In front of each of them when he is traveling in Raqia (heaven), royal servants are running with great glory and majesty just as on earth the Princes are traveling in chariots with horsemen and great armies and in glory and greatness with praise, song and honor.

CHAPTER 18

The order of ranks of the angels is established by the homage.

Rabbi Ishmael said: Metatron, the Angel, the Prince of the Presence, the glory of all heaven, said to me: (1) THE ANGELS OF THE FIRST HEAVEN, when (ever) they see their prince, they dismount from their horses and bow themselves. And THE PRINCE OF THE FIRST HEAVEN, when he sees the prince of the second heaven, he dismounts, removes the glorious crown from his head and bows himself to the ground. AND THE PRINCE OF THE SECOND HEAVEN, when he sees the prince of the third heaven, he removes the glorious crown form his head and bows himself to the ground. AND THE PRINCE OF THE THIRD HEAVEN, when he sees the prince of the fourth heaven, he removes the glorious crown form his head and bows himself to the ground. AND THE PRINCE OF THE FOURTH HEAVEN, when he sees the prince of the fifth heaven, he removes the glorious crown form his head and bows himself to the ground. AND THE PRINCE OF THE

FIFTH HEAVEN, when he sees the prince of the sixth heaven, he removes the glorious crown from his head and bows himself to the ground. AND THE PRINCE OF THE SIXTH HEAVEN, when he sees the prince of the seventh heaven he removes the glorious crown from his head and bows himself to the ground. (2) AND THE PRINCE OF THE SEVENTH HEAVEN, when he sees THE SEVENTY-TWO PRINCES OF KINGDOMS, he removes the glorious crown from his head and bows himself to the ground.

The number 70 appears as does the number 72. It is possible the difference can be explained by the 70 angels along with two leaders, such as Mikael (Michael) and Sammael. In the following section the names of the angels do not follow their function, as in the prior portion of the book. The names are obscure and it is difficult to understand their meanings. The expression "bows himself to the ground" and "bow themselves" likely indicates a complete kneeling position with the head touching the earth.

(3) And the seventy two princes of kingdoms, when they see The door keepers of the first hall in the ARABOTH RAQIA in the highest heaven, they remove the royal crown from their head and bow themselves. And The door keepers of the first hall, when they see the doorkeepers of the second Hall, they

remove the glorious crown form their head and bow themselves. The door keepers of the second hall, when they see the door keepers of the third hall, they remove the glorious crown from their head and bow themselves. The door keepers of the third hall, when they see the door keepers of the fourth Hall, they remove the crown from their head and bow themselves. The door keepers of the fourth hall, when they see the door keepers of the fifth Hall, they remove the glorious crown from their head and bow themselves. The door keepers of the fifth hall, when they see the doorkeepers of the sixth Hall, they remove the crown from their head and fall to their face. The door keepers of the sixth hall, when they see the The door keepers of the seventh hall, they remove the glorious crown from their head and bow themselves. (4) And the door keepers of the seventh Hall, when they see The Four Great Princes, the honored ones, who are appointed over the four Camps Of SHEKINA, they remove the crowns of glory from their head and bow themselves. (5) And the four great prince, when they see TAGHAS, the prince, great and honored with song (and) praise, at the head of all the children of heaven, they remove the glorious crown from their head and bow themselves. (6) And Taghas, the great and honored prince, when he sees BARATTIEL, the great prince of three fingers in

the height of Araboth, the highest heaven, he removes the
glorious crown from his head and bows himself to the ground.

*Three fingers in height – Hold your hand out at arm's length with
three fingers held out horizontally in front of your eyes. This is the
measurement.*

(7) And Barattiel, the great prince, when he sees HAMON, the
great prince, the fearful and honored, beautiful and terrible, he
who makes all the children of heaven to shake, when the time
draws near that is set for the saying of the 'Thrice Holy', he
removes the glorious crown form his head and bows himself to
the ground. For it is written (Isa.33:3): " At noise of the
confusion at the anxious preparation of the salutation of "Holy,
Holy, Holy" the people are fled; at the lifting up of yourself the
nations are scattered," (8) And Hamon, the great prince, when
he sees TUTRESSIEL, the great prince he removes the glorious
crown from his head and bows himself to the ground. (9) And
Tutresiel YHWH, the great prince, when he sees ATRUGIEL,
the great prince, he removes the glorious crown from his head
and bows himself to the ground. (10) And Aatrugiel the great
prince, when he sees NA'ARIRIEL YHWH, the great prince, he
removes the glorious crown from his head and bows himself to
the ground. (11) And Na'aririel YHWH, the great prince when

he see SAANIGIEL, the great prince, he removes the glorious crown from his head and bows himself to the ground. (12) And Sasnigiel YHWH, when he sees ZAZRIEL YHWH, the great prince, he removes the glorious crown from his head and bows himself to the ground. (13) And Zazriel YHWH, the prince, when he sees GEBURATIEL YHWH, the prince, he removes the glorious crown from his head and bows himself to the ground. (14) And Geburatiel YHWH, the prince, when he sees ARAPHIEL YHWH, the prince, he removes the glorious crown from his head and bows himself to the ground. (15) And Araphiel YHWH, the prince, when he sees ASHRUYLU, the prince, who presides in all the sessions of the children of heaven, he removes the glorious crown from his head and bows himself to the ground. (16) And Ashruylu YHWH, the prince, when he sees GALLISUR YHWH, THE PRINCE, WHO REVEALS ALL THE SECRETS OF THE LAW (Torah), he removes the glorious crown from his head and bows himself to the ground. (17) And Gallisur YHWH, the prince, when he sees ZAKZAKIEL YHWH , the prince who is appointed to write down the merits of Israel on the Throne of Glory, he removes the glorious crown form his head and bows himself to the ground. (18) And Zakzakiel YHWH, the great prince, when he sees ANAPHIEL YHWH, the prince who keeps the keys of the heavenly Halls, he removes the glorious crown from his head and bows himself to the ground. Why is he called by the name of Anaphiel? Because the shoulders of his honor and majesty and his crown and his splendor and his brilliance overshadows all the chambers of Araboth (highest heaven) of Raqia (heaven) on high even as the Maker of the World overshadows them. Regarding the Maker of the world, it is written that His glory covered the heavens, and the earth was full of His praise. The honor and majesty of Anaphiel cover all the glories of Araboth (highest heaven) the highest.

Araphiel means "Neck or Strength of God." Ashruylu means "To cause to rest / dwell." It is one of the names of the Godhead. Gallisur means, "reveal the secrets of the Law. " He reveals the reasons and secrets of the Creator. Raziel means, "Secrets of God." He hears the divine decrees. Anaphiel means "Branch of God." Zakzakiel means, "Merit of God." The glorious crowns signify honor and status.

(19) And when he sees SOTHER ASHIEL YHWH, the prince, the great, fearful and honored one, he removes the glorious crown from his head and bows himself to the ground. Why is he called Sother Ashiel? Because he is assigned to rule over the four heads of the river of fire, which are beside the Throne of Glory; and every single prince who goes out or enters before the Shekina, goes out or enters only by his permission. For the

seals of the river of fire are entrusted to him. And furthermore, his height is 7000 groups of ten-thousand parasangs. And he stirs up the fire of the river; and he goes out and enters before the Shekina to expound what is recorded concerning the inhabitants of the world. According for it is written (Dan. 7:10): "the judgment was set, and the books were opened." (20) And Sother Ashiel the prince, when he sees SHOQED CHOZI, the great prince, the mighty, terrible and honored one, he removes the glorious crown from his head and falls upon his face. And why is he called Shoqed Chozi? Because he weighs all the merits of man on a scale in the presence of the Holy One, blessed be He. (21) And when he sees ZEHANPURYU YHWH, the great prince, the mighty and terrible one, honored, glorified and feared in the entire heavenly household, he removes the glorious crown from his head and bows himself to the ground. Why is he called Zehanpuryu? Because he commands the river of fire and pushes it back to its place. (22) And when he sees AZBUGA YHWH, the great prince, glorified, revered, honored, adorned, wonderful, exalted, loved and feared among all the great princes who know the mystery of the Throne of Glory, he removes the glorious crown from his head and bows himself to the ground. Why is he called Azbuga? Because in the future he will clothe the righteous and pious of the world with garments of life and wrap them in the cloak of life, so that they can live an eternal life in them. (23) And when he sees the two great princes, the strong one and the glorified one who are standing above him, he removes the glorious crown from his head and bows himself to the ground. And these are the names of the two princes: SOPHERIEL YHWH (Sopheriel YHWH the Killer), the great prince, the honored, glorified, blameless, venerable, ancient and mighty one. (24) Why is he called Sopheriel YHWH who kills (Sopheriel YHWH the Killer)? Because he is assigned to control the books of the dead, so that everyone, when the day of his death draws near, is written by him in the books of the dead. Why is he called Sopheriel YHWH who makes alive (Sopheriel YHWH the Lifegiver)? Because he is assigned control over the books of life, so that every one whom the Holy One, blessed be He, will bring into life, he writes him in the book of life, by authority of The Divine Majesty. Perhaps he might say: "Since the Holy One, blessed be He, is sitting on a throne, they are also sitting when writing." The Scripture teaches us (I Kings 22:19, 2 Chron. 28:18): "And all the host of heaven are standing by him." They are called "The host of heaven" in order to show us that even the Great Princes and all like them in the high heavens, fulfill the requests of the Shekina in no other way than standing. But how is it possible that they are able to write, when they are standing?

This section is very important to Jewish mystics and Cabbalists in that it sets the balance within the act of judgment between mercy and justice. If one were to strip down to the barest essentials the spiritual life of a person some may conclude it is to find balance between mercy and justice. The books of life and death are records of the birth and death of individuals. This is not the same as the Book of Life referred to in the Bible, which contains the names of the righteous.

(25) It is done thusly. One is standing on the wheels of the tempest and the other is standing on the wheels of the wind of the storm. The one is clothed in kingly garments, the other is clothed in kingly garments. The one is wrapped in a mantle of majesty and the other is wrapped in a mantle of majesty. One is crowned with a royal crown, and the other is crowned with a royal crown. The one's body is full of eyes, and the other's body is full of eyes. One is looks like lightning, and the other looks like lightning. The eyes of the one are like the sun in its power, and the eyes of the other are like the sun in its power. The one's height is the height of the seven heavens, and the other's height is the height of the seven heavens. The wings of the one are as many as the days of the year, and the wings of the other are as many as the days of the year. The wings of one reach over the width of Raqia (heaven), and the wings of the other reach over the width of Raqia (heaven). The lips of one

look like the gates of the East, and the lips of the other look like the gates of the East. The tongue of the one is as high as the waves of the sea, and the tongue of the other is as high as the waves of the sea. From the mouth of the one a flame proceeds, and from the mouth of the other a flame proceeds. From the mouth of the one lightning is emitted and from the mouth of the other lightning is emitted. From the sweat of one fire is kindled, and from the sweat of the other fire is kindled. From the one's tongue a torch is burning, and from the tongue of the other a torch is burning. On the head of the one there is a sapphire stone, and upon the head of the other there is a sapphire stone. On the shoulders of the one there is a wheel of a swift cherubim, and on the shoulders of the other there is a wheel of a swift cherubim. One has in his hand a burning scroll; the other has his hand a burning scroll. The length of the scroll is 3000 times ten-thousand parasangs; the size of the pen is 3000 times ten-thousand of parasangs; the size of every single letter that they write is 365 parasangs.

Sopheriel is the prince appointed over the book of life. The name means "Scribe of God." Azbuga is a messenger. The name denoted strength, as many angelic names do. Zehanpuryu means "the face of fear." To be full of eyes is a symbol of omniscience. Eastern gates were

large, tall structures. The two symbolic uses of fire are destruction
and purification.

CHAPTER 19

Rikbiel, the prince of the wheels of the Merkaba (chariot). And
the Sacred Salutation of Holy, Holy, Holy

Rabbi Ishmael said: Metatron, the Angel, the Prince of the
Presence, said to me: (1) Above these three angels, who are
these great princes, there is one Prince, distinguished, revered,
noble, glorified, adorned, fearful, fearless, mighty, great,
uplifted, glorious, crowned, wonderful, exalted, blameless,
loved, like a ruler, he is high and lofty, ancient and mighty,
there is none among the princes like him. His name is RIKBIEL
YHWH, the great and revered prince who is standing by
Merkaba (chariot). (2) And why is he called RIKBIEL? Because
he is assigned to rule over the wheels of the Merkaba (chariot),
and they are given to his authority. (3) And how many are the
wheels? Eight; two in each direction. And there are four winds
compassing them round about. And these are their names: "the
Winds of the Storm", "the Tempest", "the Strong Wind", and
"the Wind of Earthquake." (4) And under them four rivers of

fire are constantly running and there is one river of fire on each side. And around them, between the rivers, four clouds are affixed. They are "clouds of fire", "clouds of torches", "clouds of coal", "clouds of brimstone" and they are standing by their wheels.

There is much number symbolism here. Some Eastern cultures believe there are only eight possible directions of movement. They could be looked at as north, south, east, west, up, down, in, out. Anything else must be a combination of these. Four is the number of limits and testing. Two is the number of assistance, witness, or duplicity.

(5) And the feet of the Chayoth are resting on the wheels. And between two wheels an earthquake is roaring and thunder is sounding. (6) And when the time draws near for the recital of the Song, numerous wheels are moved, the numerous clouds tremble, all the chieftains (shallishim) become afraid, and all the horsemen (parashim) become angry, and all the mighty ones (gibborim) are excited, all the host (seba'im) are frightened, and all the troops (gedudim) are fearful, all the appointed ones (memunnim) hurry away, all the princes (sarim) and armies (chayelim) are confused, all the servants (mesharetim) faint and all the angels (mal'akim) and divisions (degalim) suffer with pain. (7) And one wheel makes a sound

to be heard by the other and one Cherub speaks to another, one Chayya to another, one Seraph to another (saying) (Ps. 68:5) "Extol to him that rides in Araboth (highest heaven), by his name Jah (Yah) and rejoice before him!"

The name Jah (Yah) is a shortened and "speakable" version of YHWH or Jehovah.

CHAPTER 20
CHAYYLIEL, the prince of the Chayoth

Rabbi Ishmael said: Metatron, the angel, the Prince of the Presence, said to me: (1) Above these there is one great and mighty prince. His name is CHAYYLIEL YHWH, a noble and honorable prince, a prince before whom all the children of heaven tremble, a prince who is able to swallow up the entire earth in one moment at a single mouthful. (2) And why is he called CHAYYLIEL YHWH? Because he is assigned to rule over the Holy Chayoth and he strikes the Chayoth with lashes of fire: and glorifies them, when they give praise and glory and rejoicing and he causes them to hurry and say "Holy" "Blessed be the Glory of YHWH from His place!" (The Kedushah - Sacred Salutation of Holy, Holy, Holy).

CHAPTER 21

The Chayoth

Rabbi Ishmael said: Metatron, the angel, the Prince of the Presence, said to me: (1) The Four Chayoth correspond to the four winds. Each Chayya is as big as the space of the entire world. And each one has four faces; and each face is like the face of the East (sunrise). (2) Each one has four wings and each wing is like the tent (ceiling) of the universe. (3) And each one has faces in the middle of faces and wings in the middle of wings. The size of the faces is 248 faces, and the size of the wings is 365 wings. (4) And every one is crowned with 2000 crowns on his head. And each crown is like the rainbow in the cloud. And its splendor is like the magnificence of the circle of the sun. And the sparks that go out from every one are like the glory of the morning star (planet Venus) in the East.

CHAPTER 22

KERUBIEL, the Prince of the Cherubim.
Description of the Cherubim

Rabbi Ishmael said: Metatron, the angel, the Prince of the Presence, said to me: (1) Above these there is one prince, noble, wonderful, strong, and praised with all kinds of praise. His name is CHERUBIEL YHWH, a mighty prince, full of power and strength, a prince of highness, and Highness (is) with him, a righteous Prince, and Righteousness (is) with him, a holy prince, and holiness (is) with him, a prince of glorified in (by) thousand host, exalted by ten thousand armies (2) At his anger the earth trembles, at his anger the camps (of armies) are moved, from fear of him the foundations are shaken, at his chastisement the Araboth (highest heaven) trembles. (3) His stature is full of (burning) coals. The height is that of the seven heavens and the breadth of his stature is like the sea. (4) The opening of his mouth is like a lamp of fire. His tongue is a consuming fire. His eyebrows are like the splendor of the lightning. His eyes are like sparks of bright light. His face is like a burning fire. (5) And there is a crown of holiness upon his head on which the Explicit Name is graven, and lightning proceeds from it. And the bow of the Shekina is between his shoulders. And his sword is like lightning; and on his thighs there are arrows like flames, and upon his armor and shield there is a consuming fire, and on his neck there are coals of burning juniper wood and (also) around him (there are coals of burning juniper).

The bow can represent a rainbow but it is certainly a weapon of great power. Juniper is a symbol of strength and longevity. It was said to shelter the prophet Elijah from Queen Jezebel's pursuit. Tales in the apocryphal books tell of how the infant Jesus and his parents were hidden from King Herod's soldiers by a juniper during their flight into Egypt.

(7) And the splendor of Shekina is on his face; and the horns of the majesty on his wheels; and a royal diadem upon his head. (8) And his body is full of eyes. And wings are covering the entire of his high stature (lit. the height of his stature is all wings). (9) On his right hand a flame is burning, and on his left a fire is glowing; and coals are burning from it. And burning staves go forth from his body. And lightning is projected from his face. With him there is always thunder within thunder, and by his side there is a never ending earthquake within an earthquake. (10) And the two princes of the Merkaba (chariot) are together with him. (11) Why is he called CHERUBIEL YHWH, the Prince. Because he is assigned to rule over the chariot of the Cherubim. And the might Cherubim are given to his authority. And he adorns the crowns on their heads and polishes the diadem upon their heads (skulls). (12) He increases the glory of their appearance. And he glorifies the beauty of their majesty. And he expands the greatness of their honor. He

makes their songs of praise to be sung. He makes the strength of their beauty increase. He causes the brightness of their glory to shine forth. He makes their goodness, mercy, and lovingkindess to grow. He separates their radiance so it show even more. He makes the beauty of their mercy even more beautiful. He glorifies their upright majesty. He sings the order of their praise to establish the dwelling place of Him who dwells on the Cherubim. (13) And the Cherumim are standing by the Holy Chayoth, and their wings are raised up to their heads (are as the height of their heads) and Shekina is (resting) upon them and the bright Glory is upon their faces and songs of praise are in their mouth and their hands are under their wings and their feet are covered by their wings and horns of glory are upon their heads and the splendor of Shekina on their face and Shekina is resting on them and sapphire stones surround them and columns of fire are on their four sides and columns of burning staves are beside them. (14) There is one sapphire on one side and another sapphire on the other side and under the sapphires there are coals of burning juniper wood. (15) And a Cherub is standing in each direction but the wings of the Cherubim surround each other above their heads in glory; and they spread them to sing with them a song to him that inhabits the clouds and to praise the fearful majesty of the king of kings with their wings.

The sound coming from their wings is heard as a song. This hearkens back to a description of Lucifer, before the fall. It was said that his body had instruments made within it, which made beautiful music.

(16) And CHERUBIEL YHWH, is the prince who is assigned to rule over them. He arrays them in proper, beautiful and pleasant orders and he exalts them in all manner of exaltation, dignity and glory. And he hurries them in glory and might to do the will of their Creator every moment. Above their high heads continually dwells the glory of the high king "who dwells on the Cherubim."

Names in this section are related to the station of the angels. Chayyliel is the prince of the Chayyoth, Cherubiel or Kerubiel is the prince of the Kerubim or Cherubim, and so on.

CHAPTER 22-B

Rabbi Ishmael said to me: Metatron, the angel, the Prince of the Presence, said to me: (1) How are the angels standing on high? He said: A bridge is placed from the beginning of the doorway

Joseph B. Lumpkin

to the end, like a bridge that is placed over a river for every one
to pass over it. And three ministering angels surround it and
sing a song before YHWH, the God of Israel. And standing
before it are the lords of dread and captains of fear, numbering
a thousand times thousand and ten thousand times ten
thousand, and they sing praises and hymns before YHWH, the
God of Israel. (3) Many bridges are there. There are bridges of
fire and many bridges of hail. Also many rivers of hail,
numerous storehouses of snow, and many wheels of fire. (4)
And how many are the ministering angels are there? 12,000
times ten-thousand: six-thousand time ten-thousand above and
six (thousand times ten-thousand) below. And 12,000 are the
storehouses of snow, six above and six below. And 24 times
ten-thousand wheels of fire, 12 times ten-thousand above and
12 times ten-thousand below. And they surround the bridges
and the rivers of fire and the rivers of hail. And there are
numerous ministering angels, forming entries, for all the
creatures that are standing in the midst thereof, over against
the paths of Raqia (heaven) Shamayim. (5) What does YHWH,
the God of Israel, the King of Glory do? The Great and Fearful
God, mighty in strength, covers His face. (6) In Araboth
(highest heaven) are 660,000 times ten-thousand angels of glory
standing over against the Throne of Glory and the divisions of
flaming fire. And the King of Glory covers His face; for else the

Araboth (highest heaven) of Raqia (heaven) would be torn apart from its center because of the majesty, splendor, beauty, radiance, loveliness, brilliancy, brightness and Excellency of the appearance of (the Holy One,) blessed be He. (7) There are innumerable ministering angels carrying out his will, many kings and princes in the Araboth (highest heaven) of His delight. They are angels who are revered among the rulers in heaven, distinguished, adorned with song and they bring love to the minds of those who are frightened by the splendor of Shekina, and their eyes are dazzled by the shining beauty of their King, their faces grow black and their strength fails. (8) There are rivers of joy, streams of gladness, rivers of happiness, streams of victory, rivers of life, streams of friendship and they flow over and go out from in front of the Throne of Glory and grow large and wend their way through the gates on the paths to Araboth (highest heaven) of Raqia (heaven) at the voice of shouting and music of the CHAYYOTH, at the voice of the rejoicing of the cymbals of his OPHANNIM and at the melody of the cymbals of His Cherubim. And they grow great and go out with noise and with the sound of the hymn: "HOLY, HOLY, HOLY, IS THE LORD OF HOST; THE WHOLE EARTH IS FULL OF HIS GLORY!"

CHAPTER 22 -C

Rabbi Ishmael said: Metatron, the Prince of the Presence said to
me: (1) What is the distance between one bridge and another?
Tens of thousands of parasangs. They rise up tens of thousands
of parasangs , and the go down tens of thousands of parasangs.
(2) The distance between the rivers of dread and the rivers of
fear is 22 times ten-thousand parasangs; between the rivers of
hail and the rivers of darkness 36 times ten-thousand
paragangs; between the chambers of lightnings and the clouds
of compassion 42 times ten-thousand parasangs; between the
clouds of compassion and the Merkaba (chariot) 84 times ten-
thousand parasangs; between the Merkaba (chariot) and the
Cherubim 148 times ten-thousand parasangs; between the
Cherubim and the Ophannim 24 times ten-thousand parasangs;
between the chambers of chambers and the Holy Chayoth
40,000 times ten-thousand parasangs; between one wing (of the
Chayoth) and another 12 times ten-thousand parasangs; and
the breadth of each one wing is of that same measure; and the
distance between the Holy Chayoth and the Throne of Glory is
30,000 times ten-thousand parasangs. (3) And from the foot of
the Throne to the seat there are 40,000 times ten-thousand
parasangs. And the name of Him that sits on it: let the name be
sanctified! (4) And the arches of the Bow are set above the

Araboth (highest heaven), and they are 1000 thousands and 10,000 times ten thousands of parasangs high. Their measure is after the measure of the 'Irin and Qaddishin (the Watchers and the Holy Ones). As it is written, (Gen. 9:13) "My bow I have set in the cloud." It is not written here "I will set" but "I have set," that is to say; I have already set it in the clouds that surround the Throne of Glory. As His clouds pass by, the angels of hail turn into burning coal. (5) And a voice of fire goes down from the Holy Chayoth. And because of the breath of that voice they run (Ezek. 1:14) to another place, fearing that it could command them to go; and they return for fear that it may injure them from the other side. Therefore "they run and return." (6) And these arches of the Bow are more beautiful and radiant than the radiance of the sun during the summer solstice. And they are brighter (whiter) than a flaming fire and they are large and beautiful. (7) Above the arches of the Bow are the wheels of the Ophannim. Their height is 1000 thousand and 10,000 times 10,000 units of measure after the measure of the Seraphim and the Troops (Gedudim).

The Irin and Qaddishin are the highest ranked of all the angels. They constitute the supreme council of heaven. These angels are the twin sentinels. The Irin decrees while the Qaddishin sentences every case in the court of heaven. In Daniel 4:14 we find references. "By decree of the sentinels is this decided, by order of the holy ones, this sentence, that all who live may know that the most High rules over the kingdom of men: he can give it to whom he will, or set over it the lowliest of men. For the words rendered, "of the holy god," we read in Chaldee (in which Daniel was composed) the words elain cadisin ('-l-h-y-n q-d-y-sh-y-n) [vocalized this would be 'elahin qaddishin], which means "holy gods," not "holy God," (St. Jerome, Commentary on Daniel (1958). pp. 15-157)

CHAPTER 23

The winds are blowing under the wings of the Cherubim

Rabbi Ishmael said: Metatron, the Angel, the Prince of the Presence, said to me: (1) There are numerous winds blowing under the wings of the Cherubim. There blows "the Brooding Wind", for it is written (Gen. 1: 2): "and the wind of God was brooding upon the face of the waters." (2) There blows "the Strong Wind", as it is said (Ex.14: 21): "and the Lord caused the sea to go back by a strong east wind all that night." (3) There blows "the East Wind" for it is written (Ex. 10: 13): "the east wind brought the locusts." (4) There blows "the Wind of Quails for it is written (Num. 9: 31): "And there went forth a wind from the Lord and brought quails." (5) There blows "the Wind of Jealousy" for it is written (Num. 5:14): "And the wind of jealousy came upon him." (6) There blows the "Wind of Earthquake" and it is written (I Kings. 19: 11): "and after that the wind of the earthquake; but the Lord was not in the earthquake." (7) There blows the "Wind of YHWH" for it is written (Ex. 37: 1): "and he carried me out by the wind of YHWH and set me down." (8) There blows the "Evil Wind" for it is written (I Sam. 14: 23): "and the evil wind departed from him." (9) There blows the "Wind of Wisdom" and the "Wind of Understanding" and the "Wind of Knowledge" and the "Wind of the Fear of YHWH" for it is written (Is. 11: 2): "And the wind of YHWH shall rest upon him; the wind of wisdom and understanding, the wind of counsel and might, the wind of knowledge and the fear of YHWH." (10) There blows the "Wind of Rain", for it is written (Prov. 25: 23) "the north wind brings forth rain." (11) There blows the "Wind of Lightning", for it is written (Jer. 10: 13): "he makes lightning for the rain and brings forth the wind out of his storehouses." (12) There blows the "Wind, Which Breaks the Rocks", for it is written (1 Kings 19: 11): "the Lord passed by and a great and strong wind (rent the mountains and break in pieces the rocks before the Lord.) (13) There blows the Wind of Assuagement of the Sea", for it is written (Gen. 7 1): "and God made a wind to pass over the earth, and the waters assuaged." (14) There blows the

"Wind of Wrath", for it is written (Job1: 19): 'and behold there came a great wind from the wilderness and smote the four corners of the house and it fell." (15) There blows the "Wind of Storms", for it is written (Ps. 148: 8): "Winds of the storm, fulfilling his word." (16) And Satan is standing among these winds, for "the winds of the storm" is nothing else but "Satan" and all these winds do not blow but under the wings of Cherubim, for it is written (Ps. 18.11): "and he rode upon a cherub and flew, yes, and he flew with speed upon wings of the wind." (17) And where do all these winds go? The Scripture teaches us, that they go out from under the wings of the Cherubim and descend on the globe of the sun, for it is written (Eccl. 1:6): "The wind goes toward the south and turns around to the north; it turns around over and over in its course and the wind returns again to its route." And from the orb of the sun they return and go down on to the rivers and the seas, then up on the mountains and up on the hills, for it is written (Am. 55:13): "For lo, he that forms the mountains and creates the wind." (18) And from the mountains and the hills they return and go down again to the seas and the rivers; and from the seas and the rivers they return and go up to the cities and provinces: and from the cities and provinces they return and go down into the Garden, and from the Garden they return and descend to Eden, for it is written (Gen. 3: 8) "walking in the Garden in the wind (cool) of day." In the middle of the Garden they come together and blow from one side to the other. In the Garden they are perfumed with spices from the Garden in its most remote parts, until the winds again separate from each other. Filled with the odor of the pure spices, the winds bring the aroma from the most remote parts of Eden. They carry the spices of the Garden to the righteous and godly who in time to come will inherit the Garden of Eden and the Tree of life, for it is written (Cant 45: 16): "Awake, O north wind; and come you south; blow upon my garden and eat his precious fruits."

The same word used for "wind" is also used for "spirit." It is interesting to read the same verses using the word "spirit." It should also be noted that when certain attributes are associated with "wind," such as the wind of jealousy, it could be seen to be an agent of God, such as an angel or demon.

CHAPTER 24

The different chariots of the Holy One, blessed be He

Rabbi Ishmael said: Metatron, the Angel, the Prince of the Presence, the glory of all heaven, said to me: (1) The Holy One blessed be He, has innumerable chariots. He has the "Chariots of the Cherubim", for it is written (Ps. 18:11, 2 Sam 22: 11): "And he rode upon a cherub and did fly." (2) He has the "Chariots of Wind", for it is written: "and he flew swiftly upon the wings of the wind." (3) He has the "Chariots of the Swift Cloud", for it is written (Is.19:1): "Behold, the Lord rides upon a swift cloud:. (4) He has "Chariots of Clouds", for it is written (Ex. 19:9): "Lo, I come unto you in a cloud." (5) He has the "Chariots of the Altar", for it is written, " I saw the Lord standing upon the Altar." (6) He has the "Chariots of Ribbotaim", for it is written (Ps. 68:18): "The chariots of God are Ribbotaim; thousands of angels."

Ribbotaim appear to be used as the chariot and are a type of Cherub.

(7) He has the "Chariots of the Tent", for it is written (Deut. 31:15): "And the Lord appeared in the Tent in a pillar of cloud." (8) He has the "Chariots of the Tabernacle", for it is written (Lev. 1:1): "And the Lord spoke unto him out of the tabernacle." (9) He has the "Chariots of the Mercy-Seat", for it is written (Num. 7:89): "then he heard the Voice speaking unto him from upon the mercy-seat." (10) He has the "Chariots of Sapphire", for it is written (Ex. 24:10): "and there was under his feet a paved street of sapphires." (11) He has the "Chariots of Eagles", for it is written (Ex. 19:4): "I bare you on eagles'

wings." It is not Eagles that are not meant here but "they that fly as swiftly as the eagles." (12) He has the "Chariots of a Shout", for it is written: "God is gone up with a shout." (13) He has the "Chariots of Araboth (highest heaven)," for it is written (Ps 68 :5): " Praise Him that rides upon the Araboth (highest heaven)." (14) He has the "Chariots of Thick Clouds", for it is written (Ps. 106:3): "who makes the thick clouds His chariot." (15) He has the "Chariots of the Chayoth," for it is written (Ezek. 1:14): "and the Chayoth ran and returned." They run by permission and return by permission, for Shekina is above their heads. (16) He has the "Chariots of Wheels (Galgallim)", for it is written (Ezek. 10: 2): "And he said: Go in between the whirling wheels." (17) He has the "Chariots of a Swift Cherub," for it is written, "riding on a swift cherub." And at the time when He rides on a swift cherub, as he sets one of His feet upon his back, and before he sets the other foot upon his back, he looks through eighteen thousand worlds at one glace. And he perceives and understands and sees into them all and knows what is in all of them, and then he sets down the other foot upon the cherub, for it is written (Ezek. 48:35): " Round about eighteen thousand." How do we know that He looks through every one of them every day? It is written (Ps. 14: 2): "He looked down from heaven upon the children of men to see if there were any that understand, that seek after God." (18) He has the "Chariots of the Ophannim", for it is written (Ezek. 10:12): "and the Ophannim were full of eyes round about." (19) He has the "Chariots of His Holy Throne", for it is written (Ps. 67:8): "God sits upon his holy throne" (20) He has the "Chariots of the Throne of Yah (Jah)", for it is written (Ex. 17:16): "Because a hand is lifted up upon the Throne of Jah (Yah)." (21) He has the "Chariots of the Throne of Judgment," for it is written (Is. 5: 16): "but the Lord of hosts shall be exalted in judgment." (22) He has the "Chariots of the Throne of Glory", for it is written (Jer. 17:12): "The Throne of Glory, set on high from the beginning, is the place of our sanctuary." (23) He has the "Chariots of the High and exalted Throne", for it is written (Is. 6: 1): "I saw the Lord sitting upon the high and exalted throne."

CHAPTER 25

Ophphanniel, the Prince of the Ophannim and a description of the Ophannim

Rabbi Ishmael said: Metatron, the Angel, the Prince of the Presence, said to me: (1) Above these there is one great prince, highly honored, fit to rule, fearful, ancient and powerful. OPHAPHANNIEL YHWH is his name. (2) He has sixteen faces, four faces on each side, also a hundred wings on each side. And he has 8466 eyes, corresponding to the days of the year and sixteen on each side. (Other sources have it as: corresponding to the hours in a year.)

The number of 8466 is difficult to understand in a 365 day year. The lunar year was calculated to be 352.5 days at the time of the righting of 3 Enoch. 8466 is the number of hours in a lunar year. This makes sense and makes the alternate rendering the correct one. However, other places in the texts may refer to the number 8766, which is exact number of hours is a solar year of 365.25 days.

(3) And in those two eyes of his face, in each one of them lightning is flashing, and from each one of them burning staves are burning; and no creature is able to look at them: for anyone who looks at them is burned up instantly. (4) His height is the distance of 2500 years' journey. No eye can see and no mouth can tell of the mighty power of his strength except the King of kings, the Holy One, blessed be He. He alone can tell.

The number 2500 yields the number 7, as the digits are added together. This pattern will occur again is these types of measurements. It is a way Jewish mystics re-enforce the perfection of the template of heaven.

(5) Why is he called OPHPHANNIEL? Because he rules over the Ophannim and the Ophannim are given over to his authority. He stands every day and attends to them and makes them beautiful. And he raises them up and determines their activity. He polishes the place where they stand and makes their dwelling place bright. He even makes the corners of their crowns and their seats spotless. And he waits upon them early and late, by day and by night, in order to increase their beauty and make their dignity grow. He keeps them diligent in the praise of their Creator. (6) And all the Ophannim are full of eyes, and they are full of brightness; seventy-two sapphires are fastened to their garments on their right side and seventy-two sapphire are fastened to their garments on their left side.

Note the number 72 again, representing the nations of the world.

(7) And four carbuncle stones are fastened to the crown of every single one, the splendor of which shines out in the four directions of Araboth (the highest heaven) even as the splendor of the orb of the sun shines out in all the directions of the universe. And why is it called Carbuncle (Bare'qet)? Because its splendor is like the appearance of a lightning (Baraq). And tents of splendor, tents of brilliance, tents of brightness as of

sapphire and carbuncle enclose them because of the shining appearance of their eyes.

Carbuncle is an archaic name given to red garnet. The word occurs in four places in most English translations of the Bible. Each use originates from the Greek term Anthrax – meaning coal, in reference to the color of burning coal. A carbuncle is usually taken to mean a gem, particularly a deep-red garnet, which has no facet and is convex. In the same place in the masoretic text is the Hebrew word "nofech (no'-fekh)." In Exdodus 28:17 and again is Exodus 39:10 the carbuncle is used as the third stone in the breastplate of the Hoshen. Ezekiel 28:13 refers to the carbuncle's presence in the Garden of Eden.

CHAPTER 26

The Prince of the Seraphim.
Description of the Seraphim

Rabbi Ishmael said: Metatron, the Angel, the Prince of the Presence, said to me: (1) Over them there is one prince, who is wonderful, noble, of great honor, powerful and terrible, a chief leader and a fast scribe. He is glorified, honored and loved. (2) He is completely filled with splendor, and full of praise. He shines and he is totally full of the brightness of light and beauty. He is full of goodness and greatness. (3) His face is identical to that of angels, but his body is like an eagle's body. (4) His is magnificent like lightning, his appearance like burning staves. His beauty like sparks. His honor burns bright like glowing coal. His majesty like chashmals, His radiance like the light of the planet Venus. His image is like the Sun. His height is as high as the seven heavens. The light from his eyebrows is seven times as bright.

Chasmal is the fiery substance, which makes up the pillars on which the world rests. It is a mysterious substance or entity illuminating the heart of Ekekiel's chariot vision. Midrash Konen designated chashmal another class of angelic being.

(5) The sapphire on his head is as large as the entire universe and as splendid as the great heavens in radiance. (6) His body is full of eyes like the stars of the sky, innumerable and cannot be known. Every eye is like the planet Venus. But there are some of them like the Moon and some of them like the Sun. From His ankles to his knees they are like stars twinkling (of lightning). From his knees to his thighs is like the planet Venus, across his thighs like the moon, from his thighs to his neck is like the sun. From his neck to his head is like the Eternal Light. (7) The crown on his head is like the splendor of the Throne of

Glory. The size of the crown is the distance of 502 years'
journey. There is no kind of splendor, no kind of brilliance, no
kind of radiance, no kind of light in the universe that is not
affixed to the crown.

*As in the prior chapter, the number seven is the result of the addition
of the digits in the measurement, which in this case is 502.*

(8) The name of that prince is SERAPHIEL YHWH. And the
crown on his head, its name is "the Prince of Peace." And why
is he called by the name of SERAPHIEL YHWH? Because he is
assigned to rule over the Seraphim. And the flaming Seraphim
are under his authority. And he presides over them by day and
night and teaches them to sing, praise, and proclaim the
beauty, power and majesty of their King. They proclaim the
beauty of their King through all types of Praise and
Sanctification. (Kedushah - Sacred Salutation of Holy, Holy,
Holy). (9) How many Seraphim are there? Four, equating to the
four winds of the world. And how many wings have each one
of them? Six, relating to the six days of Creation. And how
many faces do they have? Each one of them have four faces.
(10) The height measurement of the Seraphim is the height of
the seven heavens. The size of each wing is like the span of all
Raqia (heaven). The size of each face is like the face of the East.

(11) And each one of them gives out light, adding to the splendor of the Throne of Glory, so that not even the Holy Chayoth, the honored Ophannim, nor the majestic Cherubim are able to look on it. Anyone who gazes at it would be blinded because of its great splendor. (12) Why are they called Seraphim? Because they burn (saraph) the writing tables of Satan: Every day Satan sits together with SAMMAEL, the Prince of Rome, and with DUBBIEL, the Prince of Persia, and they write down the sins of Israel on their writing tables, which they hand over to the Seraphim, so that the Seraphim can present them to the Holy One, blessed be He, so that He should eliminate (destroy) Israel from the world. But the Seraphim know the secrets of the Holy One, blessed be He. They know that He does not want the people Israel to perish. What do the Seraphim do about this? Every day they receive the tablets from the hand of Satan and they burn them in the burning fire, which is near the high and exalted Throne. They do this in order that the tablet should not come before the Holy One, blessed be He, when he is sitting upon the Throne of Judgment, judging the entire world in truth.

Satan and Sammael are not allowed to approach the throne of God, but their accusations are taken by a Seraph, who destroys the tablet with the accusations against Israel and burns it. The tablet is not

given to God, who would have to judge Israel, since the Seraph knows
God does not wish to judge or punish Israel.

Dubbiel is the guardian angel of Persia and one of the special accusers
of Israel. Dubbiel is an angel who was ranked among angels who were
said to act as guardians over the seventy nations. Dubbiel was
counted as the protector of Persia and as such defended its interests
against its enemy Israel, a role that naturally put him at odds with
the Chosen People and their special patron, St. Michael the
Archangel. Sammael is an angel whose name has been interpreted as
meaning "angel" or "god" (el) of "poison" (sam). He is the guardian
angel of Rome, another enemy of Israel. He is considered in legend a
member of the heavenly host who fell. He is equated with Satan and
the chief of the evil spirits. He is the angel of death. In this capacity he
is a fallen angel but remains the Lord's servant, or at least under His
control. As a good angel, Sammael resided in the seventh heaven,
although he is declared to be the chief angel of the fifth heaven.

Seraphim are among the highest and most splendid of the nine
accepted angelic orders as developed by the sixth-century theologian
Dionysius. They are the closest in all of heaven to the throne of God.
They are said to glow as if they are on fire so brightly they no mortal
can endure the sight..

CHAPTER 27

RADWERIEL, the keeper of the Book of Records.

Rabbi Ishmael said: Metatron, the Angel of YHWH, the Prince of the Presence, said to me: (1) Above the Seraphim there is one prince, exalted above all princes. He is more wonderful than all the servants. His name is RADWERIEL YHWH who is assigned to rule over the treasuries of the books.

Radweriel is appointed over the treasury of book of records or remembrances. (See Mal.3:16). He is an angelic scribe, fluent in reading and writing. He reads the records in the Beth Din, (house/court) of justice. This is another name for the Sanhedrin.

(2) He couriers the Case of Writings, which has the Books of Records in it, and he brings it to the Holy One, blessed be He. And he breaks the seals of the case, opens it, and takes out the books and delivers them before the Holy One, blessed be He. And the Holy One, blessed be He, receives them out of his hand and gives them to the Scribes to see so they may read them in the Great Beth (house) Din in the height of Araboth (highest heaven) of Raqia (heaven), before the household of heaven. (3) And why is he called RADWERIEL? Because from every word going out of his mouth an angel is created. He

stands in the service of the company of the ministering angels and sings a song before the Holy One, blessed be He, as the time draws near for the recitation of the Thrice Holy One.

CHAPTER 28

The 'Irin and Qaddishin (Watchers and Holy Ones)

Rabbi Ishmael said: Metatron, the Angel, the Prince of the Presence, said to me: (1) Above all these there are four great princes. Their names are Irin and Qaddishin. They are highly honored, revered, loved, wonderfully glorious, and greater than any of the heavenly children. There is none like them among all the princes of heaven (sky). There are none equal to them among any Servants. Each one is equal to all the rest of the heavenly servants put together. (2) And their dwelling is near the Throne of Glory and their standing place near the Holy One, blessed be He. The brightness of their dwelling is a reflection from the brightness from the Throne of Glory. Their face is magnificent and is a reflection of the magnificence of Shekina. (3) They are elevated by the glory of the Divince Majesty (Gebura) and praised by (through) the praise of Shekina. (4) And not only that, but the Holy One, blessed be He, does nothing in his world without first consulting them.

Only after He consults them does He perform it. As it is written (Dan. 4: 17): "The sentence is by the decree of the Irin and the demand by the word of the Qaddishin." (5) The Irin are two (twins) and the Qaddishin are two (twins). In what fashions standing before the Holy One, blessed be He? We should understood, that one Ir is standing on one side and the other 'Ir on the other side. Also, one Qaddish is standing on one side and the other on the other side. (6) And they exalt the humble forever, and they humble and bring to the ground those that are proud. They exalt to the heights those that are humble. (7) And every day, as the Holy One, blessed be He, is sitting upon the Throne of Judgment and judges the entire world, and the Books of the Living and the Books of the Dead are opened in front of Him all the children of heaven are standing before Him in fear and dread. They are in awe and they shake. When the Holy One, blessed be He, is sitting on the Throne of Judgment to execute His judgment , His garment is white as snow, the hair on his head is like pure wool and the His entire cloak is shining with light. He is covered with righteousness all over, like He is wearing a coat of mail. (8) And those Irin and Qaddishin (Watchers and Holy Ones) are standing before Him like court officers before the judge. And constantly they begin and argue a case and close the case that comes before the Holy One, blessed be He, in judgment, according for it is written

(Dan. 4. 17): "The sentence is by the decree of the 'Irin and the demand by the word of Qaddishin."

This section explains the function of the Irin and Qaddishin. They are two pairs of angels forming the apex of angelic power. They are the holy councilors and they have authority over all things terrestrial. They are judge and executioner. Another tradition has the Irin and Qaddishin as two classes of angels but many in number. Yet, they seem to come in sets of two each, like twins. Again, this may represent the balance of mercy and justice always sought in heaven.

(9) Some of them argue the case and others pass the sentence in the Great Beth Din (Great House of the Sanhedrin) in Araboth (the highest heaven). Some of them make requests in the presence of the Divine Majesty and some close the cases before the Most High. Others finish by going down and confirming the judgement and executing the sentences on earth below. According for it is written (Dan. 4. 13, 14): "Behold an Ir and a Qaddish came down from heaven and cried aloud and said , "Chop down the tree, and cut off his branches, shake off his leaves, and scatter his fruit: let the beasts escape from under it, and the fowls from his branches." (10) Why are they called Irin and Qaddishin (Watchers and Holy Ones)? Because they sanctify the body and the spirit with beatings with fire on the

third day of the judgment, for it is written (Hos. 6: 2): "After two days will he revive us: on the third he will raise us up, and we shall live before him."

Irin and Qaddishin or ministering spirits receive men from the angel of death. They judge him with angels arguing for him. This takes two days. On the third day they pass judgment. The sentence is based on the man's character and how closely he followed the Torah. They beat them accordingly.

CHAPTER 29

Description of a class of angels

Rabbi Ishmael said: Metatron, the Angel, the Prince of the Presence, said to me: (1) Each one of the Angels has seventy names corresponding to the seventy languages (nations) of the world. And all of them are based upon the name of the Holy One, blessed be He. And every several name is written with a flaming pen of iron on the Fearful Crown (Kether Nora), which is on the head of the high and exalted King.

Metatron was said to have names based upon the names of God. Fearful Crown refers to the crown of a sitting king, thus God.

(2) And each one of them projects sparks and lightning. Each one of them is covered with horns of splendor all over. Lights shine from each of them, and each one is surrounded by tents of brilliance so that not even the Seraphim and the Chayoth who are greater than all the children of heaven are able to look at them.

CHAPTER 30

The 72 princes of Kingdoms and the Prince of the World are at the Great Sanhedrin.

Rabbi Ishmael said: Metatron, the Angel, the Prince of the Presence, said to me: (1) Whenever the Great Beth Din (House of the Sanhedrin) is seated in the Araboth (highest heaven) of Raqia (heaven) there no one speaks. No mouth opens for anyone in the world except those great princes who are called YHWH by the name of the Holy One, blessed be He. (2) How many are those Princes are there? Seventy-two princes of the kingdoms of the world besides the Prince of the World who pleads in favor of the world before the Holy One, blessed be He. Every day at the appointed hour the book with the records of all the deeds of the world is opened. For it is written (Dan. 7:10): " The judgment was set and the books were opened."

The highest classes of angels are marked with the Tetragrammaton. Each nation has its own angel appointed to guard and plea for its cause. What is odd about this is the equal and universal appeal to justice. There is no difference in how the court is conducted between Gentile or Jew. In this scenario, Metatron is the Prince of the world.

CHAPTER 31

The attributes of Justice, Mercy and Truth

Rabbi Ishmael said: Metatron, the Angel, the Prince of the Presence, said to me: (1) At the time when the Holy One, blessed be He, is sitting on the Throne of Judgment, Justice is standing on His right and Mercy on His left and Truth in front of His face, (2) then man (Some sources say "wicked man" but this is to be read as mankind) enters before Him for judgment, then , a staff comes out from the splendor of Mercy towards him and it stands in front of the man. Then man falls upon his face, and all the angels of destruction are fearful and they shake before him. For it is written (Is. 16:5): "And with mercy shall the throne be established, and he shall sit upon it in truth."

The fundamental balance of justice and mercy is only possible through truth, including the truth of what the real intent of the person being judged was. This is only possible with God. The angels of destruction are there to execute man but Mercy stops them and makes the angels fear. The wording of the verse makes this point unclear.

CHAPTER 32

The execution of judgment on the wicked. God's sword

Rabbi Ishmael said: Metatron, the Angel, the Prince of the Presence, said to me: (1) When the Holy One, blessed be He, opens the Book, half of it is fire and half of it is flames. Then the angels of destruction go out from Him continually to execute the judgment on the wicked by His sword, which is drawn from its sheath and it shines like magnificent lightning and pervades the world from one end to the other. For it is written (Is. 66:16): "For by fire will the Lord plead by His sword with all flesh." (2) And all those who come into the world fear and shake before Him, when they behold His sharpened sword like lightning from one end of the world to the other, and sparks and flashes of the size of the stars of Raqia (heaven) going out from it; according for it is written (Deut. 32: 41): If I whet the lightning of my sword."

CHAPTER 33

The angels of Mercy, of Peace, and of Destruction are by the Throne of Judgment.

Rabbi Ishmael said: Metatron, the Angel, the Prince of the Presence, said to me: (1) At the time that the Holy One, blessed be He, is sitting on the Throne of Judgment, then the angels of Mercy are standing on His right, the angels of Peace are standing on His left and the angels of Destruction are standing in front of Him. (2) And there is one scribe standing beneath Him, and another scribe standing above Him. (3) And the glorious Seraphim surround the Throne on all four of its sides with walls of lightning. And the Ophannim surround them with burning staves all around the Throne of Glory. And clouds of fire and clouds of flames surround them to the right and to the left. The Holy Chayoth carry the Throne of Glory from below. Each one uses only three fingers. The length of each fingers is 800,000 and 700 times one hundred, and 66,000 parasangs. (4) And underneath the feet of the Chayoth there are seven rivers of fire running and flowing. And the distance across of each river is 365 thousand parasangs and its depth is 248 thousand times ten-thousand parasangs. Its length cannot be known and is immeasurable. (5) And each river turns round in a bow in the four directions of Araboth (the highest heaven) of Raqia (heaven), and from there it falls down to Maon and is stopped, and from Maon (some sources have "Velum") to Zebul, from Zegul to Shechaqim, from Shechaqim to Raqia (heaven) to Shamayim and from Shamayim it fows on the heads of the wicked who are in Gehenna, for it is written (Jer. 23:19): "Behold a whirlwind of the Lord, even His fury, is gone, yes, a whirling tempest; it shall burst upon the head of the wicked."

Maon or Velum is the name of the first heaven. The river flows down from heaven and all of its levels, to Gehenna, which is the burning hell. Speculation on the meaning of the numbers contained in this chapter are random. In general, 3 is the number of spiritual completeness, and 8 is the number of judgment. The number of man and his shortcomings is 6. The number 7 represents spiritual perfection. 5 represents grace and spirit.

CHAPTER 34

The different concentric circles around the Chayoth consist of fire, water, hailstones.

Rabbi Ishmael said: Metatron; the Angel, the Prince of the Presence, said to me: (1) The hoofs of the Chayoth are surrounded by seven clouds of burning coals. The clouds of burning coals are surrounded on the outside by seven walls of flames. The seven walls of flames are surrounded on the outside by seven walls of hailstones (stones of El-gabish, Ezek.13: 11, 13, 28: 22). The hailstones are surrounded on the outside by boulders (stones) of hail. The boulders (stones) of hail are surrounded on the outside by stones of "the wings of the tempest." The stones of "the of the winged tempest" are surrounded by the outside by flames of fire. The chambers of the whirlwind are surrounded on the outside by the fire and water. (2) Around the fire and the water are those who sing the "Holy." Around about those who sing the "Holy" are those who sing the "Blessed." Around about those who sing the "Blessed" are the bright clouds. The bright clouds are surrounded on the outside by coals of burning juniper wood. There are thousands of camps of fire and ten thousand hosts of flames. And between every camp and every host there is a cloud, so that they may not be burned by the fire.

The stones of hail are made of the two opposite substances of fire and ice. This, like the reference to fire and water, represent a balance of forces which, if applied within the spiritual realm, brings blessings.

CHAPTER 35

The camps of angels in Araboth (the highest heaven) of Raqia (heaven). Angels performing the Kedushah (Sacred Salutation of Holy, Holy, Holy)

Rabbi Ishmael said: Metatron, the Angel, the Prince of the Presence, said to me: (1) 506 (Other sources have 496) thousand times ten-thousand camps has the Holy One, blessed be He, in the height of Araboth (the highest heaven) of Raqia (heaven). And each camp is composed of 496 thousand angels.

The Gematria for 506 is "kingdom" and for 496 it is "kingdoms."

 (2) And every single angel is as tall as the width of the great sea; and the appearance of their face is like the appearance of lightning. Their eyes are like lamps of fire, and their arms and their feet were the color of polished brass and when they spoke words their voice roared and sounded like the voice of a multitude of them. (3) They all stand before the Throne of

Glory in four rows. And the princes of the army are standing at the beginning of each row. (4) Some of them sing the "Holy" and others sing the "Blessed." Some run as messengers while others stand in attendance. For it is written (Dan. 7: 10): "Thousands of thousands ministered unto Him, and ten thousand times ten thousand stood before Him. The judgment was set and the books were opened."

The singing or chanting of "Holy, Holy, Holy" is returned by the phrase, "Blessed be Thou and blessed is the name of the Lord for ever and ever."

(5) When the time nears and the hour comes to say the "Holy", first a whirlwind from before the Holy One, blessed be He, goes out and bursts on the camp of Shekina and there arises a great noise and confusion among them. For it is written (Jer. 30: 23): "Behold, the whirlwind of the Lord goes forth with fury, a continuing commotion." (6) At that moment thousands of thousands of them are changed into sparks, thousands of thousands of them ignite into burning staves, thousands of thousands flashes, thousands of thousands burst into flames, thousands of thousands change into males, thousands of thousands change into females, thousands of thousands burst into winds, thousands of thousands burst into burning fires,

thousands of thousands burst into flames, thousands of thousands turn into sparks, thousands of thousands turn into chashmals of light; until they take upon themselves the yoke of the kingdom of heaven, the high and lifted up, of the Creator of them all with fear, dread, awe, and trembling, with commotion, anguish, terror and trepidation. Then they are changed again into their former shape to have the fear of their King before them always, as they have set their hearts on saying the Song continually, for it is written (Is. 6:3): "And one cried unto another and said Holy, Holy, Holy."

The phrase, "…thousands of thousands change into males, thousands of thousands change into females …" is suspect and may have been added later. The idea of taking onto oneself the yoke of heaven may refers to the fact that the angels are reciting the "Holy" and "Blessed" discourse, which means they understand and acknowledge the ways of heaven and the place and power of God. Judgment comes accordingly.

CHAPTER 36

The angels bathe in the river of fire before they recite the Song

Rabbi Ishmael said: Metatron, the Angel, the Prince of Presence, said to me: (1) At the time when the ministering angels desire to sing (the) Song, (then) Nehar di-Nur (the stream of fire) rises with many "thousand thousands and ten-thousand ten-thousands" (of angels) of power and strength of fire (the intensity of the radiant fire of the angels flows) and it runs and passes under the Throne of Glory, between the camps of the ministering angels and the troops of Araboth (highest heaven). (2) And all the ministering angels first go down into Nehar di-Nur (stream of fire), and they dip themselves in the fire and dip their tongue and their mouth seven times; (2Kings 5:14) and after that they go up and put on the garment of Machaqe Samal and cover themselves with cloaks of chashmal (the zenith of heaven) and stand in four rows over near the side of the Throne of Glory, in all the heavens.

No meaning for the term Machaqe Samal could be found.

CHAPTER 37

The four camps of Shekina and their surroundings

Rabbi Ishmael said: Metatron, the Angel, the Prince of the Presence, said to me: (1) In the seven Halls four chariots of Shekina are standing. Before each one stands the four camps of

Shekina. Between (or behind) each camp a river of fire is continually flowing. (2) Between (or behind) each river there are bright clouds surrounding them, and between (or behind) each cloud there are pillars of brimstone erected. Between one pillar and another there stands flaming wheels, which surround them. And between one wheel and another there are flames of fire all around. Between the flames there are storehouses of lightning. Behind the storehouses of lightning there are the wings of the Wind of the Storm. Behind the wings of the Wind of the Storm are the chambers of the tempest. Behind the chambers of the tempest there are winds, voices, thunder, and sparks emitting from sparks and earthquakes within earthquakes.

The original intent of the verse may have been to draw a picture of the rivers running in concentric circles through the heavens and beside the river, in rows are clouds, lightning, and wind.

CHAPTER 38

The fear in heavens at the sound of the "Holy" is appeased by the Prince of the World

Rabbi Ishmael said: Metatron, the Angel, the Prince of the Presence, said to me: (1) At the time, when the ministering angels sing (the Thrice) Holy, then all the pillars of the heavens and their sockets shake, and the gates of the Halls of Araboth (the highest heaven) of Raqia (heaven) are shaken and the foundations of Shechaqim and the universe are moved, and the orders (secrets) of Maon and the chambers of Makon quiver, and all the orders of Raqia (heaven) and the constellations and the planets are distressed. The orbs of the sun and the moon rush away and run out of their pattens and run 12,000 parasangs and the wish to throw themselves down from heaven, (2) because of the roaring voice (sound) of their song, and the noise of their praise and the sparks and lightning that proceed from their faces. For it is written (Ps. 77: 18): "The voice of your thunder was in the heaven (the lightning illuminated the world, the earth trembled and shook)." (3) Until the Prince of the World calls them, saying; Be quiet in your place! Do not fear because of the ministering angels who sing the Song before the Holy One, blessed be He." As it is written (Job. 38: 7): "When the morning stars sang together and all the children of heaven shouted for joy."

As the appointed times approached to sing the Holy, Holy, Holy, all of heaven became anxious. Metatron quieted them and gave them focus.

CHAPTER 39

The explicit names fly from the Throne.

Rabbi Ishmael said: Metatron, the Angel, the Prince of the Presence, said to me: (1) When the ministering angels sing the "Holy" then all the explicit names that are engraved with a flaming iron pen on the Throne of Glory go flying off like eagles, each with sixteen wings. And they surround and hover around the Holy One, blessed be He, on all four sides of the place of His Shekina. (2) And the angels of the host, and the flaming Servants, the mighty Ophannim, the Cherubim of the Shekina, the Holy Chayoth, the Seraphim, the Er'ellim, the Taphsarim, the troops of burning fire, the armies of fire, the flaming hosts, and the holy princes, adorned with crowns, clothed in kingly majesty, wrapped in glory, tied with high honor, fall on their faces three times, saying: "Blessed be the name of His glorious kingdom for ever and ever."

Taphsarim are the troupes of flames. Er'el, more commonly referred to in the plural as "the Erelim", are a rank of angels in Jewish Kabbala (Cabbalah) and mythology. The name is seen to mean "the valiant/courageous." They are generally seen as the third highest rank of divine beings/angels below God. The description in the verse seems to say that letters fly off of the Torah like eagles when it is burned.

CHAPTER 40

The ministering angels rewarded and punished.

Rabbi Ishmael said: Metatron, the Angel, the Prince of the Presence, said to me: (1) When the ministering angels say "Holy" before the Holy One, blessed be He, in the proper way, then the servants of His Throne, the attendants of His Glory, go out with much happiness from under the Throne of Glory. (2) And each one carries in their hands thousands and ten thousand times ten thousand crowns of stars, similar in appearance to the planet Venus, and put them on the ministering angels and the great prince who sing the "Holy." They place three crowns on each one of them: one crown because they say "Holy", and another crown, because they say "Holy, Holy", and a third crown because they say "Holy, Holy, Holy, is the Lord of Hosts." (3) But in the moment that they do not sing the "Holy" in the right order, a consuming fire flashes out from the little finger of the Holy One, blessed be He, and descends into the middle of their ranks, which is divided into 496 thousand parts corresponding to the four camps of the ministering angels, and the fire burns up in a single moment those who did not say the "Holy" correctly. For it is written (Ps. 92:3): "A fire goes before him and burns up his adversaries round about." (4) After that the Holy One, blessed be He, opens

His mouth and speaks one word and creates other new ones like them to replace them. And each one stands before His Throne of Glory, signing the "Holy", as it written (Lam. 12:23): "They are new every morning; great is your faithfulness."

Here we see the full extent of the phrase, "taking on the yoke of heaven." One is rewarded for proper worship and ceremony or annihilated if God disapproves. The text indicates that all of the angels in the offending group are destroyed. Angels are created, nullifying the six days of the creation of everything.

CHAPTER 41
Letters engraved on the Throne of Glory created everything.

Rabbi Ishmael said: Metatron, the Angel, the Prince of the Presence, said to me: (1) Come and see the letters by which the heaven and earth were created. These are the letters by which were created the mountains and hills. These are the letters by which were created the seas and rivers, these are the letters by which were created the trees and herbs, these are the letters by which were created the planets and the constellations, these are the letters by which were created the globe of the earth and the orb of the moon and the orb of the sun, as well as Orion, the Pleiades and all the different luminaries of Raqia (heaven) were created. (2) These are the letters by which were created the Throne of Glory and the Wheels of the Merkaba (chariot) , the letters by which were created the necessities of the worlds, (3) the letters by which were created wisdom, understanding, knowledge, prudence, meekness and righteousness by which the entire world is sustained. (4) And I walked by his side and he took me by his hand and raised me up on his wings and showed me those letters, all of them, that are engraved with a flaming iron pen on the Throne of Glory. Sparks go out from them and cover all the chambers of Araboth (the highest heaven).

Jewish tradition has it that God and angels spoke Hebrew, and thus all things came into existence when God spoke them into existence in Hebrew. It is a very short leap of logic to assume the written word would have the same power and effect. This means within the various combinations of the 22 Hebrew letters all things were created and are sustained.

CHAPTER 42

Opposites kept in balance by several Divine Names

Rabbi Ishmael said: Metatron, the Angel, the Prince of the Presence, said to me: (1) Come and I will show you, where the waters are suspended in the highest place, where fire is burning in the midst of hail, where lightning flashes forth from out of the middle of snowy mountains, where thunder is roaring in the heights of the skies, where a flame is burning in the burning fire, and where voices make themselves heard within (in spite of) thunder and earthquake.

The balance indicated herein reminds one of a Zen koan – "See the sun in the midst of the rain. Scoop clear water from the heart of the fire." This chapter reveals a fundamental truth. All things are created in heaven by His word, sustained by His word, and reflected in the lower world where we live only after being created in heaven.

(2) Then I went to his side and he took me by his hand and lifted me up on his wings and showed me all those things. I saw the waters suspended on high in Araboth (the highest heaven) of Raqia (heaven) by the power of the name YAH EHYE ASHER EHYE (Jah, I am that I am), and their fruits (rain) was falling down from heaven and watering the face of the world, for it is written (Ps. 104:13): "(He waters the mountains from his chambers:) the earth is satisfied with the fruit of your

work." (3) And I saw fire and snow and hail that were mingled together within each other and yet were undamaged. This was accomplished by the power of the name ESH OKELA (consuming fire). For it is written (Deut. 55: 24): "For the Lord, your God, is a consuming fire." (4) And I saw lightning flashing out of mountains of snow and yet the lightning was not extinguished, by the power of the name YA SUR OLAMIM (Jah, the everlasting rock). For it is written (Is. 26: 4): "For Jah, YHWH is the everlasting rock." (5) And I saw thunder and heard voices that were roaring within flames of fire and they were not silenced. This is accomplished by the power of the name EL-SHADDAI RABBA (the Great God Almighty) for it is written (Gen. 17:1): "I am God Almighty." (6) And I saw a flame glowing in the middle of burning fire, and yet it was not devoured. This was done by the power of the name YAD AL KES YAH (the hand upon the Throne of the Lord.) For it is written (Ex. 17: 16): " And he said: for the hand is upon the Throne of the Lord." (7) And I looked and saw rivers of fire within of rivers of water and they were not extinguished. All of this was done by the power of the name OSE SHAlOM (Maker of Peace) for it is written (Job 25: 2): "He makes peace in high places." For he makes peace between fire and water, and between hail and fire, and between the wind and cloud, and between earthquakes and sparks.

CHAPTER 43

The abode of the unborn spirits and of the spirits of the righteous dead

Rabbi Ishmael said: Metatron said to me: (1) Come and I will show you where the spirits of the righteous are that have been created and those that have returned, and the spirits of the righteous that have not yet been created (born). (2) And he lifted me up to his side, took me by his hand and sat me near the Throne of Glory by the place of the Shekina; and he revealed the Throne of glory to me, and he showed me the spirits that have been created and had returned as well as those who were flying above the Thorne of Glory in front of the Holy One, blessed be He. (3) After that I went to interpret the following verse of Scripture and I found what is written (Isa. 57: 16: "for the spirit clothed itself before me .") It refers to the spirits that have been created in the chamber of creation of the righteous and that have returned before the Holy One, blessed be He; (and the (His) words.) "The souls I have made" refers to the spirits of the righteous that have not yet been created in the chamber (GUPH).

Within the entire book of 3 Enoch, this chapter could be the most important to all "Children of the book," Jews, Christians, and

Moslems. *The story of creation has God creating everything in six days. Everything must also include all of the souls that are ever to be born. These souls are housed in a chamber near the throne of God, called the Guph (Guf). This chapter tells us the souls of the righteous are housed.*

The righteous souls are housed in the Guph, waiting to be clothed in flesh for their incarnation. But if the righteous souls are here, where are the unrighteous souls kept? If there were another place where the unrighteous souls are kept the distinction would indicate predestination. If the character of the soul is already determined and they are stored accordingly then how is the determination made? Are we created as righteous and unrighteous beings? Does God simply look ahead and see us as we are to be?

As the next two chapters unfold, we see hints that the Guph may not be the place where all of the souls are housed but possibly it is where the souls of the righteous are conducted to be clothed in flesh and dispatched to earth through birth. The wicked soul finds his home in Sheol. If this were true it would still indicate predestination or foreknowledge are at work.

Mystical writings, such as the Zohar, describe God as a burning flame from where sparks fly outward. These sparks are the souls of the Jewish people. When these sparks return to the primal flame, time will come to an end. Another tradition states that when the Guph is emptied time will end.

Souls leaving the Guph are born and return to God after death.

CHAPTER 44

Metatron shows Rabbi Ishmael the abode of the wicked and the intermediate in Sheol.

Rabbi Ishmael said: Metatron, the Angel, the Prince of the Presence, said to me: (1) Come and I will show you the spirits of the wicked and the spirits of those in between (intermediate) where they are standing, and the spirits of those in between (intermediate), where they go down, and the spirits of the wicked, where they go down.

Now we know there are three classes of souls: the righteous, the intermediate – those in between, and the unrighteous. The obvious questions are, where were the souls of the "intermediates" kept and from where were they dispatched? Are these the souls of the "lukewarm?"

(2) And he said to me: The spirits of the wicked go down to Sheol by the hands of two angels of destruction: ZAAPHIEL and SIMKIEL. (3) SIMKIEL is assigned to rule over the intermediate to support them and purify them because of the

great mercy of the Prince of the Place (The Divine Majesty). ZAAPHIEL is assigned to rule over the spirits of the wicked in order to cast them down from the presence of the Holy One, blessed be He, and from the magnificence of the Shekina, and he casts them into Sheol, to punish them in the fire of Gehenna with rods of burning coal. (4) And I went by his side, and he took me by his hand and pointed them all out to me. (5) And I saw the faces of children of men and the way they looked. Their bodies were like eagles. And not only that but the color of the complexion of the intermediate was like pale grey because of their deeds. They were stained until they become cleansed from their iniquity in the fire.

It is interesting to note this indirect reference to Purgatory in a Jewish book written between the second and fifth centuries A.D.

(6) And the color of the wicked was like the bottom of a pot (burned black) because of the wickedness of their deeds. (7) And I saw the spirits of the Patriarchs Abraham, Isaac, and Jacob and the rest of the righteous, whom they have brought up out of their graves and who have ascended to Heaven. And they were praying before the Holy One, blessed be He, saying in their prayer: "Lord of the Universe! How long will you sit upon your Throne like a mourner in the days of his mourning

with your right hand behind you and not deliver your children
and reveal your Kingdom in the world? And how long will you
have no pity upon your children who are made slaves among
the nations of the world? Your right hand is behind you. Why
do you not stretch out the heavens and the earth and the
heavens of the highest heavens? When will you have
compassion?"

*The right hand is the symbol of power and authority. To have the
right hand behind your back means you are not using the power or
authority available to you.*

(8) Then the Holy One, blessed be He, answered every one of
them, saying: "Since these wicked commit sins on and on, and
transgress with sins again and again against Me, how could I
deliver my great Right Hand when it would mean their
downfall would be caused by their own hands.

*The reason God does not bring judgment upon the world is because
many Jews were among the unrepentant sinners. He wishes to await
their return to him before judging them. This is the ultimate mercy.*

(9) In that moment Metatron called me and spoke to me: "My
servant! Take the books, and read their evil deeds!" Then I took

the books and read their deeds and there were 36 transgressions to be found written down regarding each wicked one and besides that they have transgressed all the letters in Torah, for it is written (Dan. 55: 11): "Yea, all Israel have transgressed your Law." It is not written, "for they have transgressed from Aleph to Taw (A to Z) 36 (40) statutes have they transgressed for each letter?

Some sources have "40 statues." The number "40" is the number of severe trials and testing. The implication of the verse is that the souls have broken 40 major laws and many minor ones.

(10) Then Abraham, Isaac and Jacob wept. Then the Holy One, blessed be He said to them: "Abraham, my beloved, Isaac, my Elect one, Jacob, my firstborn, how can I deliver them from among the nations of the world at this time?" And immediately MIKAEL (Michael), the Prince of Israel, cried and wept with a loud voice and said (Ps. 10:1): "Why stand you afar off, O Lord?"

CHAPTER 45

Past and future events recorded on the Curtain of the Throne.

Rabbi Ishmael said: Metatron said to me: (1) Come, and I will show you the Curtain of The Divine Majesty which is spread before the Holy One, blessed be He. On it are written all the generations of the world and all their deeds (actions/doings), both what they have done and what they will do until the end of all generations. (2) And I came, and he showed it to me pointing it out with his fingers like a father who teaches his children the letters of Torah. And I saw each generation and within the generations I saw the rulers, the leaders, the shepherds, the oppressors (despots), the keepers, the punisher, the counselors, the teachers, the supporters, the bosses, the presidents of academies, the magistrates, the princes, the advisors, the noblemen, and the warriors, the elders, and the guides of each generation.

In the ancient world, these represent all major groups that have influence over the lives of people.

(3) And I saw Adam, his generation, their deeds (actions/doings) and their thoughts, Noah and his generation, their deeds and their thoughts, and the generation of the flood, their deeds and their thoughts, Shem and his generation, their deeds and their thoughts, Nimrod and the generation of the confusion of tongues, and his generation, their deeds and their

thoughts, Abraham and his generation, their deeds and their thoughts, Isaac and his generation, their deeds and their thoughts, Ishmael and his generation, their deeds and their thoughts, Jacob and his generation, their deeds and their thoughts, Joseph and his generation , their deeds and their thoughts, the tribes and their generation, their deeds and their thoughts, Amram and his generation, their deeds and their thoughts , Moses and his generation, their deeds and their thoughts, (4) Aaron and Mirjam their accomplishments and actions, the princes and the elders, their works and deeds, Joshua and his generation, their works and deeds, the judges and their generation, their works and deeds, Eli and his generation, their works and deeds, Phinehas, their works and deeds, Elkanah and his generation, their accomplishments and actions, Samuel and his generation, their works and deeds, the kings of Judah with their generations, their works and their doing, the kings of Israel and their generation, their accomplishments and actions, the princes of Israel, their accomplishments and actions; the princes of the nations of the world, their accomplishments and actions, the heads of the councils of Israel, their accomplishments and actions; the heads of the councils in the nations of the world, their generations, their accomplishments and actions; the rulers of Israel and their generation, their accomplishments and actions; the noblemen of Israel and their generation, their works and their deeds; the noblemen of the nations of the world and their generations, their accomplishments and actions; the men of reputation in Israel, their generation, their accomplishments and actions; the judges of Israel, their generation, their accomplishments and actions; the judges of the nations of the world and their generation, their accomplishments and actions; the teachers of children in Israel, their generations, their accomplishments and actions: the teachers of children in the nations of the world, their generation, their accomplishments and actions; the interpreters) of Israel, their generation, their accomplishments and actions; the interpreters of the nations of the world, their generation, their accomplishments and actions; (5) and all the fights and wars that the nations of the world worked against the people of Israel in the time of their kingdom. And I saw Messiah, the son of Joseph, and his generation and their accomplishments and actions that they will do against the nations of the world. And I saw Messiah, the son of David, and his generation, and all the fights and wars, and their accomplishments and actions that they will do with Israel both for good and evil. And I saw all the fights and wars that Gog and Magog will fight with Israel in the days of Messiah, and all that the Holy One, blessed be He, will do with them in the time to come.

This is the first mention of two Messiahs. However, the dual functions of the Messiah can be seen as the impetus to this idea. The Messiah is seen as a peacemaker and teacher, who brings mercy. The Messiah is also seen as a warrior, destroyer, and bringer of justice. One comes in peace and the other is determined to do war to avenge God and Israel. It appears the Messiah, son of David, is truculent compared to the son of Joseph, who will be killed for his attempt to make peace. Christians believe the same Messiah will perform both functions because he came as peacemaker and teacher but will return from heaven as the warrior of God. The text here indicates there will be two separate Messiahs.

(6) And all the rest of all the leaders of the generations and all the works of the generations both in Israel and in the nations of the world, both what is done and what will be done hereafter to all generations until the end of time all were written on the Curtain of The Divine Majesty. And I saw all these things with my eyes; and after I had seen it, I opened my mouth in praise of The Divine Majesty saying, (Eccl. 8:4, 5): "For the King's word has power and who may say unto Him, What do you do? Whoever keeps the commandments shall know no evil thing." And I said: (Ps. 104: 24) "O Lord how manifold (multi-colored/multifaceted) are your works!"

Rabbi Ishmael was shown all of the deeds and works of mankind for all generations. This implies predestination or foreknowledge. The reader must decide for himself or herself.

CHAPTER 46

The place of the stars shown to Rabbi Ishmael

Rabbi Ishmael said: Metatron said to me: (1) Come and I will show you the distance between the stars that are standing in the Raqia (heaven), for they stand there night after night in fear of the Almighty and The Divine Majesty. I will show you where they go and where they stand. (2) I walked by his side, and he took me by his hand and pointed out all of them to me with his finger. And they were standing on sparks of flames around the Merkaba (chariot) of the Almighty, The Divine Majesty. What did Metatron do? At that moment he clapped his hands and chased them off from their place. Then they flew off on flaming wings, rose and fled from the four sides of the Throne of Merkaba (chariot), and as they flew he told me the names of ever-single one. As it is written, (Ps. 137:4) "He tells the number of the stars; he gives them all their names", teaching, that the Holy One, blessed be He, has given a name to each one of them. (3) And by the authority of RAHATIEL they enter in a numbered order to Raqia (heaven) ha-shamayim (the second of the seven heavens) to serve the world. And they go out in numbered order to praise the Holy One, blessed be He, with songs and hymns, for it is written (Ps. 19: 1): "The heavens declare the glory of God." (4) But in the age to come the Holy One, blessed be He, will create them anew. For it is written (Lam. 52: 23): "They are new every morning." And they open their mouth and sing a song. Which is the song that they sing? (Ps. 8:3): "When I consider your heavens."

Rahatiel is the angelic ruler of the stars and constellations. The Ophannim is the class of angels that move the celestial sphere. Stars were considered by many cultures to be spiritual entities, or angels. This was a Babylonian concept that was absorbed. It is in this light that the stars would sing. They leave the second heaven and proceed through the heavens to the seventh heaven where they end their journey at the throne.

CHAPTER 47
Metatron shows Rabbi Ishmael the spirits of punished angels.

Rabbi Ishmael said: Metatron said to me: (1) Come and I will show you the souls of the angels and the spirits of the servants that served, whose bodies have been burned up in the fire of The Divine Majesty of the Almighty, that projects from his little finger. And they have been made into burning and glowing coals in the midst of the river of fire (Nehar di-Nur). But their spirits and their souls are standing behind the Shekina. (2) Whenever the angel servants sing a song at a wrong time or they sing what was not appointed to be sung they are burned and consumed by the fire of their Creator and by a flame from their Maker from the rooms of the whirlwind. The fire blows on them and drives them into the river of fire (Nehar di-Nur). There they become mountains of burning coal. But their spirit and their soul return to their Creator, and all are standing behind their Master. (3) And I went by his side and he took me by his hand, and he showed me all the souls of the angels and the spirits of the attending servants who were standing behind the Shekina and were standing on the wings of a whirlwind with walls of fire all around them. (4) At that moment Metatron opened the gates of the walls within which they were standing behind the Shekina for me to see. And I raised my eyes and I saw them. I saw what of every one of the angels looked like and I saw their wings were like birds made out of flames. And it looked as if they were fashioned from burning fire. In that moment I opened my mouth in praise of The Divine Majesty and said (Ps. 92: 5): "How great are your works, O Lord."

The river of fire or Nehar di-Nur is presented here as a place of resurrection of the angels since their bodies were burnt but the spirit continues and ends up again with God. However, this idea is contradicted in most Jewish mystic writings. It is possible the text here is somehow corrupted or missunderstood.

CHAPTER 48 - A

Rabbi Ishmael sees the Right Hand of the Most High

Rabbi Ishmael said: Metatron said to me: (1) come, and I will show you the Right Hand of The Divine Majesty, which He keeps behind Him because of the destruction of the Holy Temple; from which all kinds of splendor and light shine forth and by which the 955 heavens were created; and whom not even the Seraphim and the Ophannim are permitted to experience until the day that salvation shall arrive.

God became inactive because of the destruction of the temple between March and September of 70 A.D. and onward. Why God would choose the sacking of his temple to mark his quiescence might be understood by looking at the reason given for the destruction. If the Jewish people believed themselves to be the only chosen people of God then God must be their protector. To have a heathen army come in and defeat them so soundly, looting and destroying the temple of the God that was supposed to protect them brought into question their position in the divine scheme. Since the fault could not be with God, it must have been with his people. The Jewish nation must have failed God by falling away from Him or sinning badly enough to cause God to turn them over to their enemy. Since this would be a great and grievous sin, God has chosen not to become active, since that would mean having to judge His apostate people. He awaits his people to return to Him in a righteous state.

(2) and I went by his side and he took me by his hand and showed me the Right Hand of The Divine Majesty, with all types of praises, joyous singing. No mouth can articulate its worth, and no eye can look at it because of its greatness, and dignity and its majesty, and splendid beauty. (3) Not only that, but all the souls of the righteous who are counted worthy to see the joy of Jerusalem are standing by it, praising and praying before it three times every day, saying (Is. 51: 9): "Awake, awake, put on strength, O arm of the Lord" according for it is written (Is. 63: 12): "He caused his glorious arm to go at the right hand of Moses." (4) In that moment the Right Hand of

The Divine Majesty was weeping. And there flew out from its five fingers, five rivers of tears and fell they flowed down into the great sea and it shook the entire world. For it is written (Is. 24: 19,20): "The earth is utterly broken, the earth is totally dissolved, the earth is moved greatly, the earth shall stagger like a drunken man and shall be moved back and froth like a hut, five times corresponding to the fingers of His Great Right Hand. " (5) But when the Holy One, blessed be He, saw that there is not a righteous man in that generation, and no pious man on the entire earth, and no men doing justice, and that there is no one like Moses, and no intercessor like Samuel who could pray before The Divine Majesty for the salvation and deliverance of His Kingdom, His great Right Hand was revealed in the entire world that that He put it out from Himself again to work great salvation by it for Israel, (6) then the Holy One, blessed be He, will remember His own justice, favor, mercy and grace, and He will deliver His great Arm by himself, and His righteousness will support Him. For it is written (Is. 59: 16): "And he saw, that there was no man" that is like Moses who prayed countless times for Israel in the desert and averted the Divine decrees from them — "and he wondered why there was no intercessor" — like Samuel who entreated the Holy One, blessed be He, and called unto Him and He answered him and fulfilled his desire, even if it did not fit into the Divine plan. For it is written (I Sam. 12: 17): "Is it not wheat-harvest today? I will call unto the Lord." (7) And not only that, but He joined fellowship with Moses in every place, for it is written (Ps. 99: 6): "Moses and Aaron among His priest." And again it is written, (Jer. 15: 1) "Though Moses and Samuel stood before Me" (Is. 63: 5): "Mine own arm brought salvation unto Me." (8) The Holy One, blessed be He said at that time, "How long do I have to wait for the children of men to obtain salvation according to their righteousness for My power and authority? For My own sake and for the sake of My worthiness and righteousness will I deliver My power and authority and by it I will redeem my children from among the nations of the world. For it is written (Is. 48: 11): "For My own sake will I do it. For how should My name be profaned."

At this point, God has waited as long as he wished for Israel to come back to Him in righteousness by their own power. He has decided to take them back from the heathen nations.

(9) In that moment the Holy One, blessed be He, will reveal His Great Power and Authority (Arm) and show it to the nations of the world. Its length is the length of the entire world and its width is the width of the world. And its splendor looks like the splendor of the sunshine in its power in the summer solstice.

(10) Then Israel will be saved from among the nations of the world. And Messiah will appear unto them and He will bring them up to Jerusalem with great joy. And not only that but they will eat and drink for they will glorify the Kingdom of Messiah, of the house of David, in the four corners of the world.

This is the time, not for the Messiah of the house of Joseph, but for the Messiah of the house of David. This is the time of war and leadership of the nation in a physical sense.

And the nations of the world will not prevail against them, for it is written (Is. 52: 10): "The Lord has made bare His holy arm in the eyes of all the nations; and all the ends of the earth shall see the salvation of our God." And again (Deut. 32: 12): "The Lord alone did lead him, and there was no strange god with him." (Zech. 14: 9): "And the Lord shall be king over all the earth."

"Heaven" is the number 955 using Gematria. The meaning seems to be that of all heavens and all worlds.

CHAPTER 48 - B

The Divine Names that go forth from the Throne of Glory and pass through the heavens and back again to the Throne.

Many of the names are not decipherable. Attempting to place the letters into any kind of Latinized form or alphabet made the meanings even more obscure. For this reason, the names that could be interpreted with any certainty were listed. Those that yielded only meaningless letters were marked with only a dash.

These are the seventy-two names written on the heart of the Holy One, Blessed be He: Righteousness, - , Righteous (one) -, Lord of Host, God Almighty, God, YHWH - - - Living (one) - Riding upon the Araboth (highest heaven), - Life Giver - King of Kings, Holy One - - Holy, Holy, Holy, - - - Blessed be the Name of His glorious kingdom for ever and ever, - - Complete, King of the Universe, - - The beginning of Wisdom for the children of men, - -. Blessed be He who gives strength to the weary and increases strength to them that have no might, (Is. 40:29) that go forth adorned with many flaming crowns with many flames, with innumerable crowns of chashmal (celestial substance), with many, many crowns of lightning from before the Throne of Glory. And with them there are hundreds of hundreds of powerful angels who escort them like a king with trembling and dread, with amazement and shivering, with honor and majesty and fear, terror, greatness and dignity, and with glory and power, with wisdom and knowledge and with a pillar of fire and flame and lightning — and their light is as lightning flashesof light — and with the likeness of the chashmal (the substance of heaven). (2) And they give glory to them and they answer and cry before them, " Holy, Holy, Holy." And they lead them in a single line through every heaven as powerful and honorable princes. And when they bring them all back to the place of the Throne of Glory, then all the Chayoth by the Merkaba (chariot) open their mouth in praise of His glorious name, saying: "Blessed be the name of His glorious kingdom for ever and ever."

CHAPTER 48 - C

An Enoch-Metatron piece.

(1)"I seized him, and I took him and I appointed him" — that is Enoch, the son of Jared, whose name is Metatron (2) and I took him from among the children of men (5) and made him a Throne over near and beside My Throne. What is the size of that Throne? Seventy-thousand parasangs all of fire. (9) I committed to him 70 angels symbolizing the nations of the world and I gave into his authority all the household above and below. (7) And I imparted to him Wisdom and Intelligence more than all the angels. And I called his name "the LESSER YAH", whose name is by Gematria 71.

To refresh memory, Gematria was the ancient art of numerology. Each letter is given a number, usually determined by where it occurs in the alphabet. Numbers go from one to nine, then from ten to ninety, and, if there were enough letters, from one hundred to nine hundred. However, there are only 22 letters. Numbers are then summed. When the numbers are added they total seventy-one.

And I arranged all the works of creation for him. And I made him more powerful than all the ministering angels. (3) He gave Metatron—that is Enoch, the son of Jared— the authority over all the storehouses and treasuries, and appointed him over all the stores (reserves) in every heaven. And I assigned the keys of each store into him. (4) I made him the prince over all the princes and a minister of the Throne of Glory and the Halls of Araboth (the highest heaven). I appointed him over the Holy Chayoth for him to open their doors of the Throne of Glory to me, to exalt and arrange it, and I gave to him wreathe crowns to place upon their heads. I sent him to the majestic Ophannim, to crown them with strength and glory. I sent him to the honored Cherubim, to clothe them in majesty covered with radiant sparks, to make them to shine with splendor and bright light over the flaming Seraphim, to cover them with highness. I sent him to the Chashmallim of light, to make them radiant with light and to prepare the seat for me every morning as I sit upon the Throne of Glory. I have given him the secrets above and below, which are the heavenly secrets and earthly secrets so that he can praise and magnify my glory in the height of my power). (5) I made him higher than all. The height of his stature stood out in the midst of all who are of high of stature. I made seventy thousand parasangs. I made his Throne great by the majesty of my Throne. And I increased its glory by the honor of My glory. (6) I transformed his flesh into torches of fire, and all the bones of his body into burning coals; and I made his eyes look like lightning, and the light of his eyebrows as a light that will never be quenched. I made his face as bright as the splendor of the sun, and his eyes like the splendor of the Throne of Glory.

The description of Metatron is that of an angel and specifically a Seraphim, who is a fiery creature. A wreathe means victory.

(7) I made his clothing honor and majesty, beauty and highness. I covered him with a cloak and a crown of a size of

500 by 500 parasangs and this was his diadem. And I put My honor, My majesty and the splendor of My glory that is on My Throne of Glory upon him. I called him the "LESSER YHWH," the Prince of the Presence, the Knower of Secrets:. I revealed every secret to him as a father and as a friend, and all mysteries I spoke to him in truth. (8) I set up his throne at the door of My Hall that he may sit and judge the heavenly household on high. And I made every prince subject to him, so that they will receive his authority and perform his will. (9) I took Seventy names from my names and called him by them to enhance his glory. I placed Seventy princes into his hand so that he can command them to do my laws and obey my words in every language. And the proud will be brought to the ground by his word, and by the speech of his mouth he will exalt the humble to high places. He is to strike kings by his speech, to turn kings away from their own plans, and he is to set up the rulers over their dominion for it is written (Dan. 51: 21): "and he changes the times and the seasons, "and to give wisdom unto all the wise of the world and understanding and knowledge to all who understand (Dan. 51: 21): "and knowledge to them that know understanding." He is to reveal to them the secrets of my words and to teach them the command of my judgment in righteousness.

God is the God of the universe. He is the God of all. His names are infinite. Names reveal power, authority, personality traits, and character. Metatron is given authority over the nations. There are 70 nations and Metatron has 70 names.

(10) It is written (Is. 55: 11): "so shall My word be that goes forth out of my mouth; it shall not return unto me void but shall accomplish that which I please." I shall accomplish that which is not written here, but " he shall accomplish. Every word and every speech that goes out from the Holy One, blessed be He, Metatron stands and carries out. And he establishes the orders of the Holy One, blessed be He. (11) "And he shall make to prosper that which I sent." I will make to prosper what is not written here but he shall make to prosper teaching, that whatever decree proceeds from the Holy One, blessed be He, concerning a man, as soon as he makes repentance, they do not execute it upon him but they execute it upon another wicked man, for it is written (Prov. 9:8): "The righteous is delivered out of trouble, and the wicked comes in his place."

If a man repents and is no longer wicked, the angels inflicts his punishment on a person who is still wicked and has not repented

(12) And not only that but Metatron sits three hours every day in the high heavens, and he gathers all the souls of those dead who died in their mothers womb, and the nursing baby who died on their mother's breast, and of the scholars who died over the five books of the Law. And he brings them under the Throne of Glory and places them in companies, divisions and classes round the Presence, and there he teaches them the Law, and the books of Wisdom, and Haggada and Tradition and completes their education for them. It is written (Is. 28: 9) "Whom will he teach knowledge? And whom will he make to understand tradition? Them that are weaned from the milk and draw from the breast."

Ancient Jews viewed learning as one way to approach God. To study the Torah is almost as good as worship and prayer. Unborn, sucklings, those who die while studying the Torah are guiltless.

CHAPTER 48 - D
The names of Metatron.

The names fall into three major categories, those which are built upon the name "El," those that are based on the name "Metatron," and those based on the name "Yah." The reader will notice the letters EL,

ON, and YAH or YA in the names. Although the text states there are 70 names, there are in fact 105 names listed. The Latinized version of the 1928 work is referenced in this list however the parsing and pronunciations are unique to this work in order to accent the holy names found within most of the 105 names..

(1)Seventy names has Metatron which the Holy One, blessed be He, took from His own name and put upon him. And these they are: 1 Yeho-EL Yah, 2 Yeho-EL, 3 Yofi-EL and 4 Yophphi-EL, and 5 Hafifi-EL and 6 Margezi-EL, 7 Gippyu-EL, 8 Pahazi-EL, 9 Hahah, 10 Pepri-EL, 11 Tatri-EL, 12 Tabki-EL, 13 Haw, 14 YHWH, 15 Dah 16, WHYH, 17 Hebed, 18 DiburiEL, 19 Hafhapi-EL, 20 Spi-EL, 21 Paspasi-EL, 22 Senetron, 23 Metatron, 24 Sogdin, 25 HadriGon, 26 Asum, 27 Sakhpam, 28 Sakhtam, 29 Mig-on, 30 Mitt-on, 31 Mot-tron, 32 Rosfim, 33 Khinoth, 34 KhataTiah, 35 Degaz-Yah, 36 Pisf-YaH, 37 Habiskin-Yah, 38 Mixar, 39 Barad, 40 Mikirk, 41 Mispird, 42 Khishig, 43 Khishib, 44 Minret, 45 Bisyrym, 46 Mitmon, 47 Titmon 48 Piskhon, 49 SafsafYah, 50 Zirkhi, 51 ZirkhYah 52 'B', 53 Be-Yah, 54 HiBhbe-Yah, 55 Pelet, 56 Pit-Yah, 57 Rabrab-YaH, 58 Khas, 59 Khas-Yah, 60 Tafaf-Yah, 61 Tamtam-Yah, 62 Sehas-Yah, 63 Hirhur-Yah, 64 Halhal-Yah, 65 BazrId-Yah, 66 Satsatk-Yah, 67 Sasd-Yah, 68 Razraz-Yah, 69 BaZzraz-Yah, 70 Harim-Yah, 71 Sibh-Yah, 72 Sibibkh-Yah, 73 Simkam, 74 Yah-Se-Yah,

75 Sibib-Yah, 76 Sabkasbe-Yah, 77 khelil-khil-Yah, 78 Kih, 79 HHYH, 80 WH, 81 WHYH, (letters in the holy YHWH) 82 Zakik-Yah, 83 Turtis-Yah, 84 Sur-Yah, 85 Zeh, 86 Penir-Yah, 87 ZihZih, 88 Galraza-Yah, 89 Mamlik-Yah, 90 Hitt-Yah, 91 Hemekh, 92 Kham-Yah, 93 Mekaper-Yah, 94 Perish-Yah, 95 Sefam, 96 Gibir, 97 Gibor-Yah, 98 Gor, 99 Gor-Yah, 100 Ziw, 101 Hokbar, the 102 LESSER YHWH, after the name of his Master, (Ex. 23: 21) "for My name is in him",103 Rabibi-EL, 104 TUMIEL, 105 Segansakkiel, the Prince of Wisdom.

(2) And why is he called by the name Sagnesakiel? Because all the storehouses of wisdom are committed in to his hand. (3) And all of them were opened to Moses on Sinai, so that he learned them during the forty days, while he remained. He learned the Torah in the seventy ways it applies to the seventy nations, and the Prophets and the seventy application of the seventy tongues, the writings in the seventy variations of the seventy tongues, the Halakas (Jewish law and ritual) in the seventy applications of the seventy nations, the Traditions in the seventy aspects of the seventy nations, the Haggadas (Passover Seder) in the seventy aspects of the seventy tongues and the Toseftas (Secondary compilation of Jewish oral laws) in the seventy aspects of the seventy tongues. (4) But as soon as the forty days were completed, he forgot all of them in one

moment. Then the Holy One, blessed be He, called
Yephiphyah, the Prince of the Law, and (through him) they
were given to Moses as a gift, for it is written (Deut. 10:4): "and
the Lord gave them to me." And after that it remained with
him. And how do we know that it remained in his memory?
Because it is written (Mal. 55: 4): "Remember the Law of Moses
my servant which I commanded unto him in Horeb for all
Israel, even my statues and judgments." 'The Law of Moses':
that is the Torah, the Prophets and the Writings, 'statues': that
is the Halakas and Traditions, 'judgments'; that is the
Haggadas and the Toseftas. And all of them were given to
Moses on high on Sinai. (5) These seventy names are a
reflection of the Explicit names and given to the name of
Metatron: seventy Names of His by which the ministering
angels call the King of the kings of kings, blessed be He, in the
high heavens, and twenty-two letters (of the Hebrew alphabet)
that are on the ring placed on his finger with which are sealed
the destinies of the high, powerful and great princes of
kingdoms and with which are sealed along with the future of
the Angel of Death, and the destinies of every nation and
tongue. (6) Metatron, the Angel, the Prince of the Presence said;
the Angel who is the Prince of the Wisdom and the Angel who
the Prince of the Understanding, and the Angel who the Prince
of the Kings, and the Angel who the Prince of the Rulers, and

the angel who is the Prince of the Glory, and the angel who is
the Prince of the high ones and of the princes, all of which are
the exalted, greatly honored ones in heaven and on earth: (7)
"YHWH, the God of Israel, is my witness that I revealed this
secret to Moses and when I did all the host all the high heavens
were enraged against me. (8) They asked me, saying, "Why do
you reveal this secret to a son of man, born of woman, who is
tainted and unclean, a man of the putrefying drop? You gave
him the secret by which heaven and earth, sea and land,
mountains and hills, rivers and springs, Gehenna of fire and
hail, the Garden of Eden and the Tree of Life were all created
and by which Adam and Eve, and the cattle, and the wild
beasts, the birds of the air, and the fish of the sea, and
Behemoth and Leviathan, and the crawling things, the snakes,
the dragons of the sea, and the creeping things of the deserts;
and Torah and Wisdom and Knowledge and Thought and the
imparted knowledge and the Gnosis of things above and of
heaven and the fear of heaven were all created. Why did you
reveal this to flesh and blood? I answered them: Because the
Holy One, blessed be He, has given me authority. And
furthermore, I have obtained permission from the high and
exalted throne, from which all the Explicit names go forth with
lightning and fire and flaming chashmallim.

Verse 7 makes a statement that when the complete gnosis or revealed knowledge was given to Moses (through Metatron) all the heavenly host was enraged at the act. This Knowledge was not even available to all the host of heaven but was given to a human. Verse 8 asks the question in a direct and insulting way. To slightly paraphrase, it asked, "Why did You give the secrets of creation to this human who was conceived by a woman, through the transfer of semen, which spoils and putrefies and then gives birth, when blood from birth and menses is considered unclean, as is the woman herself for a time after a ritual cleansing. In light of this, all the heavenly hosts consider humans to be inferior, unclean, animals. Still, God chose to transmit to Moses the secret gnosis of creation.

Behemoth is the primal unconquerable monster of the land. Leviathan is the primal monster of the waters of the sea. Ziz is their counterpart in the sky. There is a legend that the Leviathan and the Behemoth shall hold a battle at the end of the world. The two will finally kill each other, and the surviving men will feast on their meat. Behemoth also appears in the 1 Enoch, giving a description of this monster's origins there mentioned as being male, as opposed to the female Leviathan. See Job, chapter 40 for further information.

(9) But they (the hosts) were not appeased or satisfied, until the Holy One, blessed be He, scorned them and drove them away from Him with contempt and said to them: "I delight in him, and have set my love on him, and have entrusted to him and

given unto Metatron, my Servant, and I have given to him alone, for he is Unique among all the children of heaven. (10) And Metatron brought them out from his house and storehouses and gave these secrets to Moses, and Moses gave them to Joshua, and Joshua gave them to the elders, and the elders to gave them the prophets and the men of the Great Synagogue, and the men of the Great Synagogue gave them to Ezra and Ezra the Scribe gave them to Hillel the elder, and Hillel the elder gave them to Rabbi Abbahu and Rabbi Abbahu to Rabbi Zera, and Rabbi Zera to the men of faith, and the men of faith gave them to give warning and to heal by them all disease that ravaged the world, for it is written (Ex. 15: 26): "If you will diligently hearken to the voice of the Lord, your God, and will do that which is right in His eyes, and will give ear to His commandments, and keep all his statues, I will put none of the disease upon you, which I have put on the Egyptians: for I am the Lord, that heals you."

(Ended and finished. Praise be unto the Creator of the World.)

Hillel was said to be one of the greatest and wisest Rabbis.

Joseph B. Lumpkin